BUEN CAMINO

Hiking the Camino de Santiago

By

Jim and Eleanor Clem

ISBN: 978-0-9799628-0-6

Published by
James Clem
P.O. Box 598
Alpine, Ca. 91903
619-820-2395
Sore Feet Publishing

Dedication

To Deborah and Jamie

ACKNOWLEDGMENTS

WE wanted to thank Elisa Wiggins and Christina Maule for all of their help, guidance, and suggestions. They spent many hours editing this manuscript and correcting all of our mistakes.

We also wanted to thank all of the members of our family for supporting this adventure and taking care of things at home while we were gone.

W
S   N
E

Atlantic
Ocean

Santiago
Labacolla
Arzua
Palas de Rei
Portomarin
Sarria
Triacastela
O'Cebreiro

Villafranca
Molinaseca
Rabanal
Astorga

Villadangos
Leon
Mansilla de las Mulas
El Burgo Ranero

Terradillos de Templarios
Carrion
Fromista
Castrojeriz
Hornillos
Burgos

Villafranca Montes de Oca
Belorado
Santo Domingo
Najera
Navarrete
Logrono
Viana
Los Arcos
Estella
Puente la Reina
Cizur Menor
Trinidad de Arre
Zubiri
Roncesvalles, Spain
St. Jean Pied de Port, France

Spain

INTRODUCTION

DURING the late summer of 2003, my wife and I hiked 500 miles across Northern Spain on the Camino de Santiago or The Way of Saint James. For hundreds of years, this same path has been used by the faithful making the holy pilgrimage to Santiago Compostela. It was also the route used by Roman Legions, Moor and Saracen invaders, the Knights Templar, and the armies of Charlemagne and Napoleon.

The Camino de Santiago is not only a walk across the hard-packed, rocky soil of Spain, but a journey through history, religion, and western culture.

There are hundreds of books on the history of Europe and Spain, along with several good books on the history of the Camino de Santiago. I will not attempt to duplicate those scholarly works here. I will also not be so bold as to tell you what enlightenment, philosophical meaning, or religious awakening you should experience if you choose to become a pilgrim on the Camino de Santiago. What I do hope to convey is what it was like to walk the 500 miles that make up The Way of St. James.

The Forward section of this book contains information about my wife and me, the training we did in preparation for the Camino, and equipment that we used.

Each of the following chapters covers a day on the Camino. At the start of each chapter is a short statement giving the start and end points of the day, along with the mileage covered, followed by a narrative about our experience on the trail that day. My hope is that I have been descriptive enough so that you can get the feel for what it was like on the Camino.

FORWARD

Far better it is to dare mighty things, even though checkered with failure, than to take rank with those poor spirits who neither enjoy much, nor suffer much, but live in that gray twilight that knows not victory or defeat. Theodore Roosevelt

IN July of 1998, my wife showed me an article from the Sunday travel section of the San Diego Union Tribune newspaper regarding a pilgrimage known as the Camino de Santiago or The Way of Saint James. We both read the article with interest.

About ten years before, I had taken up hiking as a pastime. I had never been an athlete, but walking from point A to point B was something even I could do. In addition to hiking around San Diego County, I made yearly trips to the Grand Canyon and Mt. Whitney. I guess my lovely bride, Diddo (a nickname, real name Eleanor), got tired of hearing my stories, so after a couple of years, she joined in all of the fun.

In 1994, a friend of ours went to Africa and climbed Mt. Kilimanjaro. After hearing about his adventure, we started talking about going to Africa the following year. This decision forced us to take our hiking more seriously. After spending as much time as possible training for the Kilimanjaro trip, including a one-day up-and-down of Mt. Whitney (Diddo's first experience with high altitude), we were ready to go.

In September of 1995 we traveled to Africa with seven friends and made the five-day up-and-down climb of Mt Kilimanjaro. This trip was our first international excursion and whetted our appetite for future adventures.

The following year, we went to the Argentinean Andes and did a one-day, 18-mile trek to the base camp of Mt. Aconcagua.

We continued with the yearly trips to Grand Canyon and Mt. Whitney, along with several other mountain hikes in California and Arizona. On many of these treks, we would cover 20 to 25 miles during a hard day of hiking.

In 1999, Diddo decided that she wanted to run a marathon. This surprised me somewhat, because Diddo had never been a runner, and she was 52 years old. She set her mind on this goal, and entered and completed the 2000 San Diego Marathon. Common sense and some old back and knee injuries, prevented me from running the marathon; however I did enter and complete the course as a race walker. We both had such a good time that we did two more marathons the following two years.

As we closed in on retirement, we talked at times about the Appalachian Trail or, closer to home, the Pacific Crest Trail. The problem was that neither one of us liked the idea of carrying a huge backpack over an extended period of time.

One of the reasons we did long one-day hikes was that we could carry a small day pack and a minimum of gear. This is why the article about the Camino de Santiago caught our attention. Here was a long trek, on a dedicated trail, that would not require hauling around 60 pounds of gear. The fact that the hike was in Spain and had a deep religious and historical meaning only added to the appeal. We filed the article away but kept tossing around the idea of making the trek.

Diddo was due to retire from America West Airlines in 2000. I had a mandatory retirement date from the San Diego Police Department of June 29, 2003. Sometime in late 2000, we made the decision that we were going to do the Camino as soon as I reached my retirement date. So there it was, set in stone: in June of 2003, we were heading for Spain.

Even with the decision made, something that is three years away tends to get put on the back burner. In the interim, I tried to find any books on the Camino, of which there were few.

We joined the Friends of the Camino and started receiving their quarterly newsletter. There did not seem to be a lot of information out there. One of the first books I found was *On the Road to Santiago* by Bob Tuggle. We both devoured Tuggle's book because it was a narrative of the hike, a nuts-and-bolts look at the Camino. Just reading about the trek made us enthusiastic.

As my retirement came closer, the pressure really started to build. It became very apparent that we would not be able to take off in June. In early March, we talked and agreed to put the trip off until late August.

Everything we had read said that the summer months were so crowded that, if at all possible, they should be avoided. This proved to be a smart move.

One of the reasons that we wanted to do the Camino right after I retired was that it gave both of us a project to work on. I knew that I would not have time to sit around and dwell on being retired. This worked like a charm. Months before my retirement, we were working on the Camino project. Newer books were coming out, all of which we read with interest.

Because of our long-distance hiking experience, we had a good idea of what kind of physical training we needed to do. The problem was that our prior experience was mostly with one-day, long-mileage hikes. With the Camino, we were looking at 40 days in a row! Even though we would not be carrying large backpacks, we would be carrying much more weight then we had in the past.

In addition to our regular weekend hiking trips, which ranged from six to ten miles, we started walking around the area where we live. We figured that we would each be carrying about 20 to 25 pounds, including water and food, so that became our target. If you have never carried a backpack with weight, the first time it feels like you have the weight of the world on your back. When we got comfortable with a certain weight, we would add a few pounds. After a couple of months, I was up to 35 pounds. I figured that working out with more than I would have on the Camino was a good idea.

Like any progressive workout routine, this seemed to work like a charm. What seemed like a ton of weight when we first started, say, ten pounds, felt like a feather after a couple of months. We both became very comfortable with the weight that we would be carrying on the Camino.

The only weakness in our system was that we were only walking six to ten miles every couple of days. On the Camino, we would be doing two or three times that mileage every single day, on different trail surfaces, in all types of weather. Like most people, however, we didn't have time to go out every day and hike fifteen-plus miles, so this was the best we could do.

Our other big challenge was equipment. Again, our past hiking experience gave us a leg up. I should say at this point that I will name brand names. No company sponsored our trip, and we did not receive any free equipment or compensation of any type. These are the items that worked well for us.

The first thing on our list was footwear. We both had over the years tried most of the name-brand hiking shoes. Both of us tend to like lighter footwear. I will wear light hiking boots or trail runners even on tough, rocky terrain like Mt. Whitney. My experience is that my feet feel much better with lighter equipment.

If you go to most hiking/outdoor outfitters, they tend to recommend heavier boots for any trip over a few miles in length, especially if you are going to be carrying any weight.

I was unhappy with the boots I had, so I started looking for something else. Knowing that whatever I decided on would have to last me for 500-plus miles over all types of terrain was somewhat intimidating.

I was at a local chain sporting goods store and saw a pair of Hi-Tec® boots that I thought might be good for work. I had never really taken the Hi-Tec brand seriously as a hiking boot because of the price. I figured that $29.00 boots just couldn't be that good. I couldn't believe how comfortable these boots were! I liked everything about them. The quality and workmanship seemed better than some very expensive brands, and they fit better than any of the other boots I had tried.

After wearing them to work for a couple of weeks, I decided to try them while hiking. I put them to the test many times and was always pleasantly surprised. I made my decision. I went back to the store, plunked down another $29.00, and picked up a pair that I would use on the Camino. Diddo did her own comparison and came to the same conclusion.

The only items that we added to the Hi-Tec boots were aftermarket insoles. Diddo did all of the research and came up with Sof Sole® insoles. They have a built-in arch support that seemed to really work well. We each purchased two pairs, thinking that we could alternate them over the 500 miles.

One more point about footwear. My experience is that most of the people selling shoes and boots at sporting goods or outdoor stores are not long-range hikers. They will advise you to buy boots that fit like a glove, saying that they will "break in" and conform to the shape of your feet. If you follow this advice your feet will look like hamburger after twenty miles. Years ago, I listened to this advice, and learned the hard way. I buy my hiking footwear at least one size larger than my normal shoe size. With the Hi-Tec boots, I went a size and a half. I wear a size ten and a half in a dress shoe. The Hi-Tec boots I purchased were twelve's. This gives my feet plenty of room to expand on a long hike. You should be able to spread your toes in the toe box of the boot. If they don't feel good in the store, it is only going to get worse in the field!

Socks are the next most important items. My advice is to try out some of the padded hiking/trekking socks on the market, and see what you like. I decided on Thorlo® socks. I tried these on our workout hikes and found that the extra padding and support was worth the extra money.

The biggest single problem people had on the Camino were blisters. Every day we would see our fellow pilgrims treating their feet. A good way to avoid this problem is to coat your feet with some Vaseline before you take off in the morning. This will help keep your feet dry and protect them from blisters.

As for clothing, we knew that we would be dealing with all types of weather. Any clothes that we took would have to be hand washed each day, probably in a sink, and would have to dry quickly. Light weight would also be a big factor. I have used ExOfficio® Amphi™ Convertible Pants and ExOfficio shirts for years, with good results.

I purchased three pairs of pants for the trip. These are the type of pants that the legs zip off, converting them into shorts. They also have built-in underwear like swim trunks, eliminating the need to carry several pairs of underwear. They have numerous pockets, one with a zipper that makes it a good secure place for your passport. These pants aren't cheap, but they wear like iron, are easy to wash, and dry very quickly.

I purchased two ExOfficio long-sleeve collared shirts. These also have a hidden pocket that comes in handy. They can be worn with the sleeves rolled up in hot weather. Along with these shirts, I added three ExOfficio short sleeve T-shirts and a long-sleeve CoolMax® T-shirt. All of these shirts are made of a wicking, easy-washing, fast-drying material.

The idea here is the layering of clothing. In hot weather, we wore a short- sleeve T-shirt. In cool or cold weather, we started adding layers of clothing. In really cold weather, we might be wearing just about everything in our backpacks.

A good jacket was the next item. After a lot of checking, we came up with the Mountain Hard-Wear Tempest SL Jacket. This jacket is rainproof, hooded, and has a built-in light fleece inside. It has numerous zipper pockets and rolls up into a fairly small bundle that can be stowed on the outside of your backpack. They cost about $165.00-expensive, but worth every cent.

The last big item was our backpacks. Like most hikers, we have a big box in the closet with backpacks, old and new, big and small. We wanted a pack that had a built-in hydration system that would carry at least 100 ounces of water. While looking at various packs, Diddo tried on a Kelty® Arrowhead "W" backpack. The "W" stands for women. The straps are arranged in a more comfortable position for a woman's body. As soon as she put it on, she fell in love with it. It has 1900 cubic inches of volume and has a bladder/tube hydration system, so that solved that problem.

I had an old Kelty Redwing that I have carried everywhere from Africa to South America. I loved the pack, but it was getting old and did not have a hydration system. As luck would have it, Kelty now makes the same pack, with the bladder. It has 2900 cubic inches of volume.

To the packs, we each added a fanny pack that could be worn in front when the backpack was on, or by itself later in the day when we were not wearing the backpack.

The other item worth talking about is a sleeping bag. We purchased REI® brand 40-degree lightweight bags because we knew the weather would be on the warmer side. These bags are inexpensive, very light, and easy to pack. About the only time we needed them was when we stayed in an *albergue.*

All of the gear we took on the trip performed well. We are still wearing the pants, shirts, and boots, even after all of the miles we put on them. The only thing that we would add is another pair of insoles.

In addition to the above items, we took the following:

Guidebook	Hat
Walking Stick (collapsible)	Sunglasses
Sandals (To wear at the end of the day)	Sun Screen
Flashlight-Headlamp	Toiletry Items
Swiss Army Knife	Sewing Kit
Extra Shoelaces	Extra Glasses
Camera and Film	Extra Batteries
Notebook and Pen	Moleskin
Lightweight Long Johns	

A few other items worth mentioning: Across Spain on the Camino de Santiago are places to stay for free or for a very small donation. The common term for these places is *Albergue*. Sometimes you will hear them referred to as *Refugios*. They are operated either by the church, the municipal government, Camino organizations, or private concerns. They are spaced every six miles or so, sometimes closer. We generally found them to be clean, well equipped, and well managed.

As the Camino de Santiago has become more popular, the *albergue* system has become overburdened and overcrowded. This is especially true during the spring, summer, and fall. It is a first-come, first-serve system, meaning that if you arrive much after noon, you might be sleeping on the floor, if you are lucky.

In 2003, over 74,600 pilgrims were awarded the Compostela. Forty percent of the pilgrims were women, 60% men. 1512 of the pilgrims were from the United States. Only 7,670 pilgrims started the Camino in St. Jean Pied de Port. The largest group, 10,300, started in Sarria.

Early on in our hike, we decided to stay in hotels or hostels to avoid this problem. The cost of a room with a bathroom is inexpensive and well worth the money. Keep in mind that the terms "hostel", *pension*, and *meson* in Europe refer to an establishment similar to a hotel and do not mean a communal type accommodation.

There are some areas of the Camino where you may not have a choice and will have to stay in an *albergue*. Plan on being there early!

ATM's are all over Spain, and obtaining money from them is as easy as it is at home. Once we were tuned into this, we did not carry as much cash as we thought we would have to. Credit cards were also very easy to use, especially at hotels.

Needless to say, Spain is a very modern country, and any supplies that you forgot to bring or run out of on the Camino, can easily be purchased while you are on the trail.

****

In late June, I walked out of the San Diego Police Department Headquarters building for the last time. Needless to say, this was a very bittersweet experience. I loved every minute of the 35 years that I served with the police department. I also knew that after all of those years of fistfights, gunfights, knife fights, high-speed chases, undercover work, high-risk search warrants, back injuries, neck injuries, knee injuries, long hours, and days away from home, that it was time to turn the job over to a younger crowd.

By mid-August, we were as ready to go as we would ever be.

CHAPTER 1

San Diego, California to Miami, Florida

2300 Miles

Carpe Diem! (Seize the Day)

ON Wednesday, August 20, 2003, after all of the planning, equipment testing, training, and emotional up and downs, we found ourselves at the San Diego airport, waiting to board a 1:25 p.m. flight to Las Vegas, where we would catch the 3:35 p.m. flight to Miami.

We were going to stay with my brother and sister-in-law who live in Miami until our flight to Madrid, on Sunday. We were traveling stand-by on Diddo's flight benefits which, thank God, were part of her retirement package. There are more flights to Spain from Miami, and leaving from there gave us a chance to visit family.

Another benefit was that a friend and fellow Professor of my brother's at Florida International University, Dr. Guillermo Grenier, has done the Camino three times. He kindly agreed to meet with us and give us a firsthand account.

It was great to finally talk to someone who had done the Camino, not just once, but three times. Guillermo briefed us for more than two hours and answered all of our questions. Some of his most valuable tips were not about the trail, but how we would feel on the trail. Guillermo told us that we would develop a routine of waking up in the morning, getting ready, and hitting the trail. He said that we would walk until early afternoon, find a place to stay, wash clothes, take a shower, eat, maybe have something to drink, and then get ready for the next day.

He also said that even though we would be walking through history, we would rarely stop because we would want to keep going and reach our destination.

His other bit of wisdom was to not make any big decisions for the first seven to ten days. He explained that it takes that long to get used to being on the trail, and that after ten days, it becomes part of your life. This proved to be very good advice, especially during the first few days when we were tired, our feet were sore, we were soaking wet, standing in mud, and thinking, "What am I doing here?"

One of the things that Diddo and I had agreed to do was to stop trying to push and pressure this trip. We decided to just get going, and let the journey happen. I really hoped that we could adopt this attitude. There had been so much going on in the last year.

I felt that we both needed to relax and start enjoying the trip for the right reasons. I thought that a large part of the trip would be to experience the entire journey. Taking delays, changes in plans, bad weather, and everything else the Camino threw at us as just part of the experience of being a pilgrim.

One of the rules we decided on was to not use the word "problem," or to think of things as problems. Learn to accept things that happen as just being part of the Camino. I know that this sounds somewhat lame, because if you break your leg, that is a problem. This attitude, however, did help us to accept some of the minor hardships that we experienced when we were out on the trail. Kind of a "don't sweat the small stuff" attitude.

CHAPTER 2

Miami, Florida, USA to St. Jean Pied de Port, France

4600 Miles

BECAUSE we were flying stand-by, we listed ourselves on both of the evening flights from Miami to Madrid. We were told that the earlier flight at 5:30 p.m. was very crowded, but with luck we might get on.

We wound up making the early flight, but we did not have seats together. I had a center seat, and Diddo had an aisle seat on the other side of the plane. A French woman was sitting next to me. I had seen her in the boarding area and noticed that she did not speak any English or Spanish, and that she was having a lot of trouble with the boarding instructions. She kept getting in line before her row was called.

I asked her if she spoke English or Spanish, to which she replied, "No." I then asked the flight attendants if they spoke any French, to which they replied, "No." Diddo and two female flight attendants came over to talk to the French woman. I told them in English and Spanish that the woman only spoke French. Diddo and the two flight attendants started speaking Spanish to the woman anyway, trying to explain that Diddo wanted to change seats with her. The woman was answering in French, explaining I assumed, that she did not understand Spanish. I gave up and just started to watch this multilingual conversation. The French woman finally got up, grabbed her stuff, and went over to the seat that Diddo had been assigned. Diddo grabbed her stuff and took the seat next to me. Somehow, it all worked out.

We landed in Madrid on Monday morning at 8:30. We missed the first flight to Pamplona, so we were going to have a long wait for the afternoon flight. The Madrid airport was a mad house. We got confirmed seats for the Pamplona flight at 4:30 in the afternoon.

We needed to get something to eat, so we wandered around until we found a sandwich/coffee counter. We ordered our first meal in Spain! Airport food, but not too bad.

We found the general area where our flight to Pamplona would leave (they don't list the gates until about an hour before flight time) and then just grabbed a place to sit down. The rest of the day we just read, slept on a bench, and did nothing. Very boring.

Our plan at this point was to get to Pamplona, grab a hotel for the night, and try to figure out how we would get from Pamplona to St. Jean Pied de Port, France, the next day.

At 4:30 p.m. we boarded an Iberia Airlines flight for Pamplona. It was only a one-hour flight, so we were in Pamplona by 5:30 p.m. The airport was smaller then I expected.

We headed to the baggage area to wait for our one checked bag. An older woman from Denmark, Marie, approached us and asked if we were pilgrims. She was headed to Roncesvalles and wanted to know if she could share a cab with us. This seemed like a good idea. It was still daylight, so we decided to forgo staying in a hotel in Pamplona and head out for St. Jean Pied de Port. If we could find a cab to take us, we were ready to go.

After retrieving our gear bag, all three of us headed out to the curb. From checking on the Internet, I knew that the Radio Cab Company would take us all the way to St. Jean Pied de Port. When we got to the curb, I noticed that every cab there was a Radio Cab. A new Mercedes cab pulled to the curb. We inquired about the trip to Roncesvalles and St. Jean. We conversed back and forth in Spanish, English, and sign language until we figured out that the fare would be 30 euros each for Diddo and me to get to St. Jean Pied de Port, France. There would be an additional 20-euro charge for Marie to be dropped off at Roncesvalles. We took the deal. We loaded everything into the trunk of the big Mercedes, and we were on our way.

Our driver was Jose, a nice guy who spoke very little English. Jose was a good but fast driver. He passed everything that got in front of us. He was playing American rock music on the radio. Jose gave us a running commentary on the countryside in Spanish. Marie spoke some Spanish, so she translated as much as she could.

About 45 minutes later, we arrived in Roncesvalles. We dropped Marie at the *albergue*, and said goodbye. She said that she was going to go slow, so we might run into her on the Camino. It did not look like there was much in Roncesvalles. After wishing Marie good luck, we took off for St. Jean Pied de Port.

It was a beautiful drive from Roncesvalles to St. Jean over the Pyrenees on a narrow, winding, but heavily-traveled road. We took everything in because we would be walking back this way. Jose was explaining in Spanish where the Camino was on the road and where it went off the road.

We reached St. Jean a little before 8:00 p.m. St. Jean appeared to be a very busy tourist town, with lots of people and traffic. Jose unloaded our gear, and I paid the fare plus a 10-euro tip. Marie had given us about 20 euros to cover her part. She tried to give us part of the tip, but we told her that we would cover that.

When Jose gave us our bags, he saw the black duffle and, with a concerned look, asked us in Spanish if we planned to carry the duffle all of the way on the Camino. We laughed and explained that we were going to load everything from that bag into our backpacks. He seemed relieved.

So there we were, in St. Jean Pied de Port, France, eight o'clock at night, and we didn't have a clue. We started walking around looking for a hotel. After about a block, we stopped and headed back to where Jose had dropped us off.

We had seen the Hotel Remparts just as we came into town. We decided that we better grab a room before it got too late. We went into the bar area and inquired about a double room with a bathroom. The clerk looked at the register and said that they had a room for 44 euros a night. We took it.

She showed us to the room, upstairs, above the bar/restaurant. It looked fine. We were tired from the long trip and both of us felt grungy, so I think that anything with a shower and beds would have sufficed.

The clerk explained that we were to come and go from a side door. This conversation was in French, so we were really in trouble. She told us to hang our room key on a board at the bottom of the stairs when we went out. That way they knew if we were out of the hotel and they would not lock the outside door. Not much for security, but that's their rule.

We went to the room, took showers, and washed our clothes. We went out, leaving the key on the board. There was a restaurant at the hotel, but it had just closed. We headed down to the corner where we had seen a restaurant with outside tables. After some back and forth with the manager, we got a table. We were both starved, it was getting late, and the menus were in French. The only things I understood on the menu were paella and pizza. I ordered pizza and Diddo ordered paella. The waitress explained to me rather abruptly that it took too long to make pizza. I changed my order to paella.

While we were waiting for our meal, I noticed several people who came in after us getting pizza, so I don't know what that was all about. We had a couple of beers that really hit the spot. The food came and turned out to be great. The weather was warm, and everything seemed to be going well.

We headed to the room and started the process of re-packing our gear. We had a down day to get our Pilgrim's Credentials and take a look at the trail. It would also give us a day to get over the long flight from Miami.

CHAPTER 3

August 26, 2003 Tuesday
St. Jean Pied de Port

I didn't sleep well-jet lag mixed with excitement. We had breakfast at our hotel: croissant, juice, and coffee. We then walked around town, getting our bearings.

After locating the Pilgrim's Office, we checked in and picked up our Pilgrim's Credentials. The gentleman who ran the Pilgrim's Office spoke good English. He explained the trail, the trail markings, etc. He went over the Route Napoleon but did not say anything about the "road route." When I inquired about it, he said that most people take the Route Napoleon. He said that they tell "older women" traveling alone about the road route.

The weather was very overcast, and it looked like rain. Heavy clouds were covering the mountains. Everything we had read indicated not to take the Route Napoleon if the weather was the least bit questionable. We were somewhat confused, because we were not "older women" traveling alone.

We got our credentials and took a look at the maps, photos, and everything else in the office. While we were there we met Pierre, a French Canadian who was doing the Camino. He had just retired from a newspaper in Quebec. Pierre was going to do the Route Napoleon, but was going to take two days to do it.

We decided to explore the route out of town, but we did not have our guidebook with us. This would be the last time that the book was not with us at all times. We went back through town to where the two trails split. There is a sign at that location that has a warning in French,

Spanish, German, and English. It says, "Do not take the Route Napoleon if the weather is questionable." We were more confused. We followed the arrows for the road route for a short distance. We then started back to town and somehow got lost. We eventually found the town and hotel, somewhat disheartened about our navigation skills.

We went to the room and finished packing. We headed out later to pick up some food for the trail. We purchased some salami, bread, and fruit.

We mailed postcards at the post office, where we ran into Pierre. He was just taking off for Untto, about 3 miles up the Route Napoleon. His plan was to spend the night in Untto, then do the rest of the way to Roncesvalles tomorrow. We wished him a *buen camino* and told him we would see him down the trail.

We each had packed a couple of paperback books and a small Bible for the trip. I decided to take just one of the paperbacks and the Bible. Diddo did the same. In the following days, as we read, we ripped out the pages to lighten the load. Later on, I wished that I had brought the other two books along.

We were both ready to get going, excited, wondering what it's going to be like out on the trail. In the middle of the night, I was wide awake, wondering if we had bitten off more than we could chew. I knew that the key was to get going and make the first few days. I was looking forward to getting my feet on the trail!

View of St. Jean from the Citadel

St. Jean Pied de Port

Busy street in St. Jean

Along the River Nive in town

CARNET DE PÈLERIN DE SAINT-JACQUES

"Credencial del Peregrino"

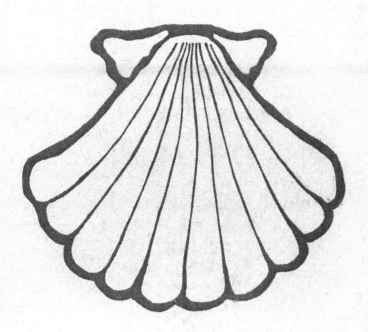

délivré par :

Les Amis du Chemin de Saint-Jacques Pyrénées-Atlantiques

☆

39, rue de la Citadelle
F.64220 SAINT-JEAN-PIED-DE-PORT
Tél. 05 59 37 05 09
aucoeurduchemin.org

N° *5729*

Pilgrim's Credential

CHAPTER 4

August 27, 2003-Wednesday-Day 1
St. Jean Pied de Port, France, to Roncesvalles, Spain

16 Miles

There are no easy days on the Camino. There are easier days, and there are harder days, but there are no easy days!

WE were up early and on the trail at 7:15 a.m. It was still dark. We followed the path that was clearly marked, but different from the guidebook. We both decided to stay with the yellow arrows, something we did the entire trip that worked well.

After about a mile, we came to a confusing intersection. There was an old man with a cane, walking the other way. We asked him if we were on the Camino. In French, he gave us an affirmative reply and told us to turn right at the T-intersection ahead. That took us back to the main highway where we would be most of the rest of the day.

We would find that almost every town, village, and city had an old man with a cane who would provide directions to us, whether we wanted them or not. Sometimes they would stop us from going one way, even if it was the marked trail. If we were going the wrong way, they would stop us and turn us around.

When we reached the main highway, we found that the trail was basically just the edge of the road. We had to be very careful about the traffic; big trucks, fast cars, people passing.

It seemed that in France and Spain, most people walked with the traffic rather than against it. They appeared to have a lot of faith in the drivers, or else they didn't care. We would always walk against traffic, unless there was a hairpin turn that we couldn't see around. There was usually no shoulder, so we would have to cross over to the other side of the road in order to see around the corner. We just had to be extra careful about vehicles coming up behind us. Once we would get around the corner, we would cross back over.

The road/trail was fairly flat, with a slight uphill for the first six miles. At that point, we crossed over the Petite Nive River and entered Spain. The village of Arneguy is located right on the border, mostly on the Spanish side. You would never know that this was the boundary between two countries. There are no border markings or guards of any type. There are several shops and restaurants here if you have not arrived too early. A small bar/café was just opening up when we arrived, so we stopped and had our first cup of Spanish coffee. Very strong, but good.

As we entered Spain, we also entered the Spanish province of Navarra. Navarra is one of three provinces that form the Basque region of Spain. Until the 16th Century, Navarra was a separate kingdom.

The Basques are a very proud and independent people, with their own history, language, and customs. They are believed to be one of Europe's oldest races.

Many signs we saw were written both in Spanish and Basque. This can be a little confusing if you don't know what is going on. For instance, Roncesvalles is also known as Orreaga; Pamplona is Iruna. Many of the TV shows were in the Basque language, which is completely different and unrelated to Spanish.

As we traveled through this region, we noticed that every village and town had a "fronton". This is a three-to four-sided court used to play "pelota" (handball) or jai alai.

After leaving Arneguy, the road/trail went uphill with a vengeance. We really had to watch traffic in both directions. At times the space between the guardrail and the road was about one foot. Because of the trees, we didn't know that on the other side of the guardrail there was a very long and steep drop-off. When we took a closer look, we realized that we were looking at the top part of the trees and that the bottom was way, way down. This took the option of jumping over the guardrail out of the picture. Most of the time, the other side of the road had almost no space between the traffic lane and a rock cliff that went straight up, so we had no place to go on that side of the road either.

When we came to these areas, we would check for traffic in both directions and just try to get through them as fast as possible. Not the best of situations, but it sure kept our minds off of the climb and our sore feet!

About two and a half miles past Arneguy, we came to the town of Valcarlos. In Valcarlos there were more shops, restaurants, and an *albergue*. The road through town was narrow, with vehicles parked on the side of the road. Valcarlos seemed like a busy little town, very pretty, with great views back toward St. Jean Pied de Port. The countryside in this area is beautiful and heavily forested.

Although we had been concerned about the weather, the day turned out to be perfect: warm, with not one cloud in the sky.

After Valcarlos, we continued on the road, steeper and steeper uphill. There was a Camino sign showing the trail going off the main road past Valcarlos. This was confusing to us because it was not marked in our guidebook.

The lesson here is that the Camino changes all of the time, and even if your map or guidebook is new, there will be some modifications that you have to adjust to.

The new section of trail was a road that went downhill to a small village or group of homes. The trail signs seemed to disappear in the middle of the village. I saw a woman in one of the homes looking out at us, so I asked her in Spanish if we were on the Camino. She gave us an affirmative reply, then barked some orders at someone named Roque inside the house. Roque came running out of the house and led us through the village to where the Camino trail continued. We thanked Roque and headed out.

The path continued somewhat level next to a stream. We seemed to be the only people on the trail. Earlier in the day, just outside of St. Jean, we had seen someone about a half mile in front of us, but had not seen him the rest of the day. We had the whole place to ourselves. We continued on this path. It eventually crossed over the stream and then started on a steep uphill to where the trail rejoined the road. The road/trail was still going steeply uphill, with lots of hairpin turns and traffic to keep us interested.

Between kilometer marker 58 and 57, the trail again went off-road. Again we headed downhill, which I didn't like because we were losing altitude that we had worked hard to gain. After a long downhill, the trail leveled out. At one point we got lost. We had been walking along, deep in our own thoughts. Diddo was following me. The danger is that you are always looking down at the trail, and sometimes you miss the trail markers that may be up on a tree or painted on a rock.

We found ourselves walking past a very old, abandoned building then into an old corral. The trail just disappeared at that location. We stopped, looked at each other, and both realized that we had missed a trail marker. The only question was how far back we had taken the wrong turn. This was not a good feeling, but it was a good lesson. You have to pay attention to the trail markings at all times. You can't afford to fall asleep at the switch.

We were in a deep ravine. I noticed what appeared to be a trail guardrail going up one side of the ravine. We started to backtrack and, to our relief, we had only passed the intersection with the Camino about a hundred yards back. We started up the right trail. This turned into the major climb of the day. What looked like a short stretch on the map turned into a long, long, uphill climb.

The weather was hot, and by this point we were beat. During the latter part of this long climb, we came around a bend and saw a body sprawled across the trail. The person didn't look like he had stopped to rest at this location, more like he had passed out or collapsed. I approached the person, a male, who appeared to be out cold. When I came abreast of him, he came to and sat up straight. I asked if he was OK. After some language back and forth, I found that he spoke perfect English. Mike, who was from Germany, was the person we had seen in front of us earlier in the day. He said that he was afraid that he was lost and became so exhausted that he lay down to rest. We assured him that he was on the right trail. He asked if he could walk with us the rest of the way.

As we walked, Mike said that he was 62 years old and a retired schoolteacher. He lives in Frankfurt, Germany. Mike said that the hike so far was much harder than he expected. Mike was wearing regular tennis shoes and only had a small bottle of water. I don't know how he was doing it because I had 100 ounces of water and had drunk most of it.

The three of us continued on the long uphill. Our map showed this trail meeting with the main road for a short distance by a dog kennel. We had been on the trail so long that I thought that maybe the trail had changed and that we might be close to the top of the grade where there is a small chapel. At one point I saw a building and the road, which seemed to confirm my theory. As we approached, I heard dogs barking everywhere and realized that we still had a ways to go.

The trail hit the road for a couple of hundred feet and then went back off- road. It was more and more uphill until we were just about to quit. We came out of the trees, at which time we could see sky, ridgeline, and the chapel. What a welcome sight! It was very windy in this high pass, but we were so happy to be at the top of the grade it didn't make any difference.

I was hoping that there would be a water fountain because I was out of water, however, no such luck. We stopped, took a couple of photos, and looked around. We noticed a tourist office by the chapel. We went over to the office, where Mike asked the clerk if he could fill up his water bottle. The clerk took the bottle, went into a back room, and returned with the bottle full. He did not seem to be very happy, however. I asked him if he could fill a small water bottle that I had, but he told me that he did not have any water. I don't know what the problem was, but Diddo still had some water we could share, and we didn't have far to go.

We started downhill, and before we knew it, we could see the monastery at Roncesvalles. What a welcome sight. On the trail, you come in from the backside, so it is a little confusing at first.

We walked into the monastery compound. The arrows took us to the *albergue* office, which was full of pilgrims who were waiting for the office to open. The room was very dark. It was about 3:30 p.m.

We were not really in the mood to hang around, so we headed to the La Posada, a small hostel-type hotel. We went into the bar area and asked the female bartender about a room. She said she would check. When she returned, she said they just had one room for four people. It had two bunk beds, and was 59 euros. Mike asked if we wanted to share a room, but we were not real keen on that idea.

Diddo and I walked over to the Hostal Casa Sabina on the main road next to the monastery. We went into the bar and asked the bartender if they had a double room with a bathroom (*doble con bano*). He said they did. It cost 42 euros. We said we would take it. He grabbed Diddo's backpack and took us up the stairs to the room. The room was small but very clean. It was such a great feeling to get into our own room with our own bathroom/shower. We were hot, tired, dirty, thirsty, and had sore feet. This was like heaven!

We learned later that Mike came in after us to get a room. However, we got the last room. He did get a good bed in a new section of the *albergue*.

We took long, hot showers, washed our clothes, and headed downstairs. It is unbelievable how much difference a hot shower and clean clothes make. I felt like a new person. We signed up for dinner at the place we were staying. We had a couple of beers that really hit the spot. We went over to the *albergue* office and had our credentials stamped. We didn't know it then, but we were setting a routine that we would follow for most of the rest of the trip.

We talked to Mike while we were having the beers. He said that he spoke good English because he had been married to an American woman when he was younger. He kept saying that we saved his life because he didn't think that he could have gone any farther when we found him on the trail.

At 7:30 p.m. we went to the dining area for dinner. We sat at a table with two women about our age who were friends. One was French Canadian, the other French. The French Canadian spoke good English.

They served the first course family style, cream of potato soup that was about the best thing we ever tasted. I had at least two bowls with bread. The main course was trout with french fries. I'm not a big trout fan because of the bones, but it was very good, and the french fries were fantastic. Wine was also included with the meal. I forget what we had for a dessert, but it was a great meal or we were just so tired and hungry it seemed that way. The cost was seven euros each.

While we were eating, I heard a big guy at the next table speaking English, but we didn't get a chance to talk to him.

We walked around to explore the trail out of Roncesvalles because we knew it would be dark when we started in the morning. This was another routine we would follow for the rest of the Camino. After making sure we knew where we were going, we headed up to the room to get ready for tomorrow's trek.

Before we went to bed I started to write in my journal. As I was doing my notes my fingers cramped up making it very difficult to write. I think that using the walking stick all day may be the cause of the problem.

We hit the sack early and slept like rocks.

Along the road in France

France or Spain ?

French/Spanish Border

Just outside of "Roque's" village

Where we lost the trail on the first day

View back toward France

The chapel at Ibaneta Pass

First view of Roncesvalles

CHAPTER 5

August 28, 2003-Thursday-Day 2
Roncesvalles to Zubiri

14 Miles

WE hit the trail at 7:15 a.m. The trail went along the road for the first several hundred yards and then headed off-road. It was still dark when we started. Sunup is between 8:00 and 8:15.

We met Nadia, a young woman from Brazil, just as we were starting the trail. She wanted to walk with us for a while. Nadia said that she was a travel agent and was married. She and her husband have one child. She told us as we were walking that the company she worked for offered her this trip. She said that her husband was at home watching their baby. She was starting in Roncesvalles, so this was her first day on the trail. She had arrived late last night and had a bad cold. Nadia spoke perfect English, so we talked as we walked along.

The trail stayed off-road for about two miles and then came back to the highway just outside of Burguete. Burguete appeared to be a nice clean town. The main street in Burguete is the highway. It is very narrow, so we really had to keep an eye on the traffic. Vehicles didn't slow down very much even though they were going through town.

Many of the pilgrims were waiting for a café/bar to open to get coffee and something to eat. Mike was there waiting. We decided to keep going. Nadia stopped to wait for the bar to open.

The trail turned back off the road in the middle of town and headed across farmland and pasture. The trail was good and fairly flat for a while. The weather was cool, clear, and nice.

The next town was Espinal, two-plus miles from Burguete. Espinal was another nice, clean-looking village. We needed to use the restroom and look for a place to get some coffee and something to eat. We found a bar in town that had just opened. We had some coffee and bread that really hit the spot. Mike caught up with us at the bar and stopped to have coffee.

After getting back on the trail, we met the American whom we had seen at dinner last night. Jerry was a big guy, in his sixties, from the Chicago area. Diddo talked to him for a while as we were walking. Jerry had battled cancer twice, most recently prostate cancer. He was doing well and wanted to do the Camino.

We climbed uphill out of Espinal, then through Viscarret (Biscarret). We crossed a small stream where we ran into Pierre and the two women we had dinner with last night. I introduced Pierre to them before we continued on.

After the village of Linzoan, we started on a very long uphill. We didn't see Mike or Jerry after that. They were walking together. The uphill led to a mountain ridge. The trail continued along this ridge for some time. It was beautiful and heavily forested.

It had become cloudy and cool, and it started to rain lightly. We stopped and put on our pack covers. After we went a little farther, the rain became heavier. We stopped again and put on our ponchos. A little farther, the bottom dropped out, and we were in a heavy thunderstorm. There was no shelter of any type, so we just kept going.

We were still on the ridge of the mountain. Good trail, but very heavy rain along with lightning and thunder. The trail was getting very muddy, and our boots were getting soaked. There was nothing to do but to keep moving forward.

At one point along the ridge trail, we were soaking wet, cold, and the rain was beating down on us. There was lightning, thunder, and mud up to the tops of our boots. We came around a corner, and there was a herd of cows with two bulls coming toward us on the trail. We stopped at first but then continued slowly. The cows took one side of the trail, and we took the other. It was a little scary at first, but no problem.

We crossed the highway, which was really exciting because of the heavy traffic whizzing by in the rain. To the left was a short road leading to the mountaintop of Alto de Erro. There were several radio towers on the peak. The trail was on the right and started downhill. This section of the trail was very muddy and slippery, with lots of slick rock. It was very confusing because the trail split several times without clear markers as to which way to go.

The rest of the way into Zubiri was a long, tough downhill for about two miles. It seemed to take forever. The rain never let up. We could see Zubiri for quite a while, but it didn't seem to get any closer.

We reached Zubiri about 2:00 p.m. and decided to look for a room for the night. We were tired, wet, muddy, and our feet were sore. Zubiri appeared to be a long highway town.

The Hosteria de Zubiri is located where the Camino enters Zubiri. The rooms were 62 euros, which seemed a little steep. They also locked the doors at midnight and didn't open them until 7:30 in the morning. We started to look around but found that the hotel was way at the other end of town, about a mile or so away. We didn't want to go that far, and it started to rain again. We headed back to the hostel and checked in. Nice clean room, with a bathroom.

After taking long hot showers and washing our clothes, we went to a little store by the hostel. We bought bread, chorizo, cheese, Ruffles® potato chips, chocolate bars, and a few other items we needed. We were both really hungry, so we headed back to the room and had a feast on all of the above.

It turned out to be a good decision to get a room here rather than continuing on. It was raining very hard with lightning and thunder. We were glad that we were inside.

Later on we walked down to the *albergue*. It is a converted school that was very crowded and didn't look all that clean. There wasn't anyone there to stamp credentials, so we had them stamped at our hostel.

We walked around a little more, but we were both tired, and it started to rain again. We headed back to the room and ate some more food. It was nice to be in a warm room. We hit the sack early and got a good night's sleep

Just outside of Burguete

Viscarret

Short break by a cool stream

View from a high ridge before Zubiri

CHAPTER 6

August 29, 2003-Friday-Day 3
Zubiri to Trinidad de Arre (Outskirts of Pamplona)

11 Miles

AFTER getting up and ready, we went downstairs and had coffee and bread. Jerry came into the dining room and came over to talk to us. Turns out he also stayed there for the night. He said that Mike walked down to the hotel at the other end of town and got a room.

We took off at 8:00. They would not let us out until 7:30 anyway. I was a little worried that this might be standard operating procedure and that we would have to deal with these late take-off times. However, this was the one and only place that had such a rule. The trail went uphill for a short distance, then leveled out for quite a while. There were some small up and downs, but nothing bad.

There is a large Magnesitas Industrial Complex, or Zona Industrial, next to the trail for the first mile or so. After that, beautiful countryside, with the trail going the same direction as the main highway. It looked like rain, and my feet hurt. We walked for a while, making one stop at the *albergue* in Larrasoana to use the restroom.

We continued on through Zuriain and Iroz. We stopped for a snack break after crossing the Rio Arga near Zabaldica. When we left home, I packed about 24 granola bars. Diddo thought I was crazy, but I thought that they might come in handy during the first few days as a trail snack. It turned out to be a good idea because during these breaks we always had something to eat. We were both beginning to feel that we were not eating enough and that we needed to increase our food intake to keep our energy level up.

As we continued, it was very cloudy, but still no rain. We reached Trinidad de Arre on the outskirts of Pamplona about noon. We made a stop at the Trinidad de Arre *albergue* to ask directions to a hotel and restaurant. It looked like a very nice place. Not many people stay there because they continue to the Pamplona *albergue*.

We got directions to the Hotel Don Carlos, which was about a mile away. It turned out to be a very nice, clean, modern hotel. The room was 63 euros.

We were starving, so we went to eat after dropping our gear off in the room. They gave us a menu that turned out to be the Menu of the Day, or Menu del Dia. We didn't understand how the menus were set up at this point. The way it works is that you pick three things off the menu: something to start (salad, soup, etc.), a main course, and dessert. Everything cost nine euros. Since we didn't have a clue, I ordered the meat and potato soup. Diddo ordered the salmon. We basically ordered one meal. The waitress made an attempt to help us, but she gave up. The meat and potato soup tasted great and was very hearty. The salmon that Diddo had was also very good. The waitress brought us a dessert that we split.

We headed back to the room, took showers, and washed our dirty clothes, after which we walked back to the *albergue* and had our credentials stamped. We made a call to our oldest daughter, Deborah, and left a happy birthday message. Later that night, I went back downstairs and called our younger daughter, Jamie, and had a nice talk with her.

Our plan for the next day was to take a short walk through Pamplona to see the city and find a place in Cizur Menor. The guidebook listed at least one hostel or hotel in Cizur Menor.

Along the trail

Crossing the bridge into Zuriain

Zuriain

Along the highway

Camino trail marker

Between Zabaldica and Trinidad

View of Trinidad de Arre

Trinidad de Arre albergue

Medieval bridge into Trinidad

CHAPTER 7

August 30, 2003-Saturday-Day 4
Trinidad de Arre to Cizur Menor

6 Miles

WE had the buffet breakfast at the hotel: rolls, bread, ham, etc. We were starting to get into the "eat everything you can eat" mode. We took off from the Don Carlos Hotel at 8:00 a.m.

We didn't have to do long mileage, so we planned on taking a slow walk through the city of Pamplona. Pamplona was our first large city in Spain. The trail crosses the Rio Arga on the Puente (Bridge) de Magdalena into the city. There is a large park along the river by the bridge.

We went through the Portal de Zumalacarregi, one of the main gates or entries into the old city through the old fortress walls. The transition is amazing. Very narrow streets and old buildings very cramped together. We walked slowly through the old town area taking in the sights, always looking for the yellow arrows. The route is well marked, but the directions in the guidebook made this easier.

Eventually we exited the old town area into the "new" section of Pamplona at the Parque Ciudadela (City Park). There are the remains of the old city fortress in and around the park. We followed the yellow arrows through the city to the outskirts, then to the road leading to Cizur Menor.

There appeared to be a lot of construction going on in Pamplona and the surrounding area. The Camino goes in and out of areas being affected by the construction, so we had to really keep an eye out for the yellow markers.

Heading out of the main city, going toward Cizur Menor, the Camino went along the side of a busy road. There was a long uphill on sidewalks into Cizur Menor. We planned to get a hotel in Cizur Menor, and according to the guidebook there was at least one.

As we entered Cizur Menor, we saw one of the *albergues*. We decided to check at the *albergue* and get information on any hotels in the area. We went inside and were greeted by the manager. After trying our Spanish, he asked us in English where we were from. Turns out that he was British, so that ended any language problem. He introduced himself as Ambrosia. We asked if he would stamp our credentials. He told us in a very matter-of-fact way that he would only stamp our credentials if we were going to stay at "his" *albergue*. This seemed to be unusual, but that was his rule. We asked about the hotel, to which he replied that there were no hotels in Cizur Menor. I told him that there was one listed in the guidebook. He seemed to get upset, and explained that he lived there, and that he knew the area very well, and that there were no hotels in the area. It turned out that the actual town of Cizur Menor is about two miles away from the Camino. There is very little in the way of stores in the general area of the Camino.

We told Ambrosia that we were going to walk around a little but that we would be back. The *albergue* was almost completely empty at that time, but we knew it would fill up quickly because Cizur Menor is one of the main stops on the Camino. A lot of pilgrims choose to stay in Cizur Menor rather than in Pamplona.

We really wanted a hotel room, so we walked around the area. Ambrosia was right. There were no hotels in the immediate area. There was another *albergue* about a block away that is really the main *albergue* for the town. We stopped there, but they were not open. An older woman, who was looking out the second story window, told us that the manager, who spoke English, would be there in 30 minutes. We did not know if we should wait or go back and check in at "Ambrosia's *albergue*." The older woman said that the *albergue* manager also had information on rooms that were available in the area.

We, or maybe I, became impatient, and decided that we better go back to Ambrosia's *albergue* and get a bed while the getting was good. We headed back and checked in with Ambrosia. The beds were four euros each. The *albergue* was fairly clean, however the flies were very thick.

There were two restroom/showers, one for men, one for women. There was also a kitchen area where Ambrosia said that he served breakfast in the morning.

We grabbed a couple of lower bunks next to each other in the first room. The place was still just about empty. We both took showers and did a quick laundry job.

We were both hungry, so we went in search of a restaurant. Right up the street was a nice-looking restaurant that was just opening for lunch. We went in and got seats. It took a while to figure out the menu, but we took a chance and ordered. First we had a great salad, then a huge piece of steak with french fries. One order was more than enough for both of us. The food was great, and we had a feast. With beers and dessert, the meal came to 35 euros.

By the time we got back to the *albergue*, the place was just about full. It was a good thing that we got there early. Buddy and Estelle, a couple from the United States took the bunks above us. Buddy was a very big guy, and every time he would jump up into the bunk above me, I thought that the thing might give way and collapse onto me. They were on an extended trip around Europe, the Camino being just part of their trip. Estelle was having some problems with her feet and seemed to be a little upset with Buddy because he wasn't paying much attention to her condition.

Their plan on the Camino was to always start early in the morning and arrive late. They said that they were from Hawaii.

Buddy talked to Ambrosia about setting up some type of service in the old church next to the *albergue* later in the evening. After overhearing this conversation, I told Diddo that I didn't want to go to some organized group deal where they were going to sit around and sing Kumbaya, so we took off to walk around the town.

There were no stores in the area, so we went to a neighborhood bar. We had a couple of beers and purchased some Ruffles potato chips and a few bags of peanuts. We headed back to the *albergue* and arrived just as the service was ending. The group was singing Kumbaya. We both had a good laugh.

We sat outside for a while, taking in the great view back toward Pamplona. It was starting to get cold, which forced us back inside the crowded *albergue*. We sat in our bunks and did our journal entries after which we read for a while.

At lights out, we tried to get some sleep. This was easier said than done because there was a lot of noise around the place. Every time Buddy moved around in his bunk, I thought that it was all over. People coming from the other rooms in the *albergue* to use the restroom would open the door, but they would not close it all the way. Every time the wind blew through the open windows, the door would rattle loudly. I wasn't expecting a good night's sleep anyway, so we took everything in stride.

The following day looked like a fairly long, hard walk, with a least one big climb. We were looking forward to getting out of the *albergue* and on to the trail.

Portal de Francia entrance into Pamplona

Medieval bridge into Pamplona

Old town Pamplona

Pamplona Town Hall

Camino through Pamplona

View back to Pamplona from Cizur Menor

Relaxing outside of the albergue in Cizur Menor

CHAPTER 8

August 31, 2003-Sunday-Day 5
Cizur Menor to Puente la Reina

14 Miles

BUDDY and Estelle were up and on their way at about 5:00 a.m. We decided that we might as well hit the road also. Because of the uncleanliness of the place, we decided to take a pass on the free breakfast.

We were on the trail before 6:00. Outside it was still very dark, cold, and looked like rain. We had to really look out for the yellow arrows. Because of new construction, the trail was not well marked.

The trail went across the valley and then started up a long, steep hill to a high ridge lined with electric-generating windmills. It really looked like rain. Clouds were completely covering the ridge. The trail going up to the ridge had great views back toward Pamplona.

An older woman from Canada whom we met on the trail yesterday was walking with us. She said that she was worried about the rain because she lost her rain poncho the day before. We had extra ponchos, so I gave her one of ours. She, like others we met on the Camino, mailed her cold weather gear ahead where she thought she would need it. This didn't seem to be a very good idea to us because you can never count on the weather.

We finally reached the high ridge, where we stopped to take a break. It was very cold and windy, but no rain. The ridge had several metal figure statues that you can see from the valley below. When we reached the ridge, we found a motor home parked on the windmill service road. There was a British gentleman serving hot coffee and cookies. He only asked for a donation to keep the service going. He was a former pilgrim.

After this refreshing and well-deserved break, we started down the other side of the ridge. As usual, the going down was as hard as the going up. The trail was very steep and rocky. The rocks made it very slippery, and we really had to watch our step. This is where the walking sticks really came in handy. They help to brake on the downhill, saving a little wear and tear on our legs and knees.

It felt good to reach the valley floor. The weather had improved on this side of the ridge. The sun was shining, and it was warm.

We decided that we needed to take more short breaks. We made a quick stop on a bench in Muruzabal. As we left Muruzabal the trail became confusing because of new road construction. The yellow arrows went one way, but temporary signs pointed a different way. We started to follow the temporary signs, but an old man with a cane came up to us and pointed out the correct route. We showed him the temporary signs, but he insisted that we go on the old trail. You could see the next village, Obanos, so we took the old man's advice and stuck to the original trail.

Obanos seemed like a nice village. We stopped for a short break in the main plaza and noticed a lot of people wearing traditional Basque attire: white shirts and pants with red scarves and red berets.

As we were leaving Obanos, an English couple stopped us and asked us if we were pilgrims. We had a short conversation with them. They said that there was a fiesta in Obanos that weekend, which was the reason for all of the activity. They thought that we might have trouble getting a hotel room in Puente la Reina because of the Obanos fiesta. We didn't want to hear this because we were looking forward to a nice room, a good hot shower, and a good meal.

We went downhill off of the mesa where Obanos is located. We then walked through a valley alongside the road. At times, the trail went through vegetable gardens. Just as we were getting hot and tired and ready for another break, we came out of the fields and saw a sign that said "Hostal." What a welcome sight.

The Hostal Jakue has both regular hotel-type rooms and an *albergue*. We opted for a regular room with a bathroom. The room was 57 euros, which by the looks of the place seemed like a good deal. The room was even better than we expected. We took good hot showers, followed by our laundry duties. We then headed down to the Hostal Jakue restaurant.

Again some confusion with the menu, but with a little help from our Spanish/English pocket dictionary, we muddled through. The meal included a salad, leg of lamb (more then enough for two people), and dessert, for 45 euros.

As had become our custom, we walked through Puente la Reina, following the Camino out of town. We had our credentials stamped at the Hostal Jakue. We were finding that just about every place we stayed at along the Camino would stamp our credentials.

We headed back to the room and kicked back, updated our journals, watched Spanish TV, and read.

Today's trek was about 12 miles, taking us six hours.

We were hoping for more good weather, but it looked like it was going to rain.

Just after leaving Cizur Menor

View toward Alto de Perdon

Getting close to the ridge

Best cup of coffee in the world

View back toward Pamplona

View to the west from Alto de Perdon

Pilgrim Monument at Alto de Perdon

Monument along the trail

Church in Obanos

Statue of St. James in Puente la Reina

CHAPTER 9

September 1, 2003-Monday-Day 6
Puente la Reina to Estella

13.5 Miles

WE hit the trail at 7:30 a.m. after a cup of coffee at the Hostal Jakue. It rained most of the night, but was clear in the morning. We walked through Puente la Reina, then over the 12th Century pilgrim's bridge that took us out of town.

It was clear and cool, good hiking weather. There were a couple of detours due to construction, followed by a couple of hard climbs in the first two or so miles. There were vineyards as far as we could see.

The trail goes through the scenic hilltop villages of Maneru and Cirauqui. We stopped in Cirauqui and bought some bread for the trail. Outside of Cirauqui we crossed an old Roman bridge. Right after that, we crossed the freeway, which brought us back to the present day. The trail continued over old Roman cobblestone roadbeds that last forever, but are very hard on the feet. Back across the freeway, this time under it, through a tunnel, then a short but steep hill into the village of Lorca.

It started to rain on and off. When it rained, we would stop and put on all of our rain gear. As soon as it stopped raining, the sun would come out and it would get warm. We would have to stop again to take everything off.

We were both very hungry. In Lorca, we went by a house that was also a small store/restaurant. We bought some cheese, potato chips, and olives. We sat outside of the store where they had plastic chairs and tables and had a feast. This seemed to give us a second wind.

Outside of Lorca I started up a section of trail, following some other pilgrims. Diddo, who was behind me, stopped and called out to me. I had taken the wrong trail. We all came back to the right trail with the exception of one guy. He continued on. I don't know where he wound up.

As the day wore on, it got hotter. We continued on through the village of Villatuerta. Again, new construction made finding the trail difficult at times.

Estella is one of those towns that came out of nowhere. We had just passed Buddy and Estelle as we crossed over a small scenic stream. We came around a corner, and there was the town of Estella.

The *albergue* is located right as you enter town. We stopped there to get our credentials stamped and check on the locations of the hotels and hostels listed in our guidebook. The *albergue* was very crowded and busy. We ran into Mike outside of the *albergue* and agreed to meet him at the main plaza for dinner.

The old town area of Estella is somewhat confusing, with narrow streets going in every direction. We got lost for a short time, but asked directions and finally found the Hostal Christina, conveniently located on the main plaza. A double room with bathroom was 40 euros. The place is very old, but clean. The only problem was that being located on the main plaza meant that it was very noisy.

We found Mike waiting for us at an outside table on the plaza. We were too early for dinner and too late for lunch, so we sat around and drank beer and had a variety of food from the tapas menu at the bar. We had *tortillas*, *bocadillos*, and olives, 37 euros for the three of us. It was a nice relaxing dinner after a long day of hiking.

Later Diddo and I did some shopping and picked up chorizo, cheese, bread, and potato chips. We also made a stop at the *farmacia* (pharmacy) and picked up some band-aid material that we could use like moleskin.

Good day today. The only problems were heat and sore feet. We did 13.5 miles in 7 hours.

Los Arcos tomorrow.

Bridge leaving Puente la Reina

Cirauqui in the distance

A closer view of Cirauqui

Camino through Cirauqui

Roman bridge

Old Roman road-hard on the feet

Old church and rest area

Church in Villatuerta

CHAPTER 10

September 2, 2003-Tuesday-Day 7
Estella to Los Arcos

13 Miles

NOT much sleep. It was very noisy most of the night. People here stay out late. We were up and away by 7:30 a.m. The trail went out of the old town area into the main city, with busy morning traffic. The trail went along streets and through alleys until we reached the outskirts of town.

On the west side of town, in the suburb of Irache, we came to the famous Fuente de Vino or "Fountain of Wine." This is a fountain that dispenses wine! There are two choices, white or red. The wine is provided free by the Bodegas winery. Because it is free, some people can't resist going crazy. We had to stand in line for a while. One guy in front of us was filling a large bottle! When it was our turn, we each filled our cups, took a small drink, and threw the rest onto the trail. A drink for us, a drink for the Camino.

Just outside of Irache, the original trail crosses to the south side of the main road. The main trail stays on the north side. Most of the pilgrims seemed to stay on the main trail. We crossed under the highway to the old, or original, trail. We seemed to have this all to ourselves. Very pretty trail through heavy forest. Up and downs, but nothing difficult. There were great views to the north. Above Villamayor de Monjardin, we could see Castillo de San Esteban clearly. During this entire section of trail, we only encountered one other pilgrim, and, of course, he came along just as Diddo decided to stop and take a pee next to the trail.

The weather was turning cold, and it started to look like rain. When we came out of the heavy forest, we encountered a sheepherder with several hundred sheep. It was very interesting to watch as he and his dogs moved their large herd from place to place.

After climbing to a high ridge along a dirt road, we decided to take a break. It was about 10:30 a.m. A snack of bread, cheese, chorizo, and, of course, Ruffles potato chips got us going again.

We continued on after the break into the village of Luquin. We had one of the biggest scares of the trip there. Just as we were walking out of Luquin on a cement road, I took a bad step. I didn't see a three-inch drop in the road surface and twisted my left ankle. Because of the weight of the pack, everything went. I fell down on my left knee and hand. My knee took most of the hit. I got up fast because I wanted to see if I had screwed anything up. The knee was scraped pretty good and bleeding a little, as was my left hand. Luckily, everything seemed to work OK.

We started walking right away because I didn't want my knee to freeze up. I guess this was just the Camino's way of reminding us that you are always just one bad step away from ending your trip. If you blow out a knee, ankle, or whatever, your trip is over-not a happy thought.

After limping out of Luquin, we crossed back over the main highway. Before rejoining the main trail, the path went through a creek bed that was overgrown with vegetation to the point that it was almost impassable. I guess not many pilgrims take this route!

As we rejoined the main trail, the rain started to fall. We stopped and put on our rain gear. As we continued on, the rain began falling harder.

The trail followed a dirt road that went through farmland. The surface of the road was rocky. I was beginning to worry about my feet because they hurt with every step. Neither one of us had blisters, but our feet hurt just from so much walking on hard, rocky surfaces.

At about noon, we wanted to stop for a break, but it was raining too hard. We did stop on a small bridge, under a tree that provided a little shelter for a minute. Shortly after the bridge, the trail split with no markings as to which way to go. We took a chance and went to the right. We were both nervous for about a quarter of a mile until we saw a yellow arrow. What a relief! We had reached that point in the day when the last thing we wanted to do was backtrack because we weren't paying attention, got lost, or took the wrong trail.

About the point where my feet were really killing me, we went over a small rise, and Los Arcos was visible just down the road. What a great sight. Our guidebook listed two *albergue*s and a Hotel Monaco. We walked through town and located the Hotel Monaco on the main road. We checked in, nice room, very clean and modern, 47 euros.

We were both starved, so after soaking our feet and taking showers, we headed to the hotel dining room. We were a little early, but the hotel owner/desk clerk/restaurant manager seated us anyway. We ordered the pilgrim's menu, 12 euros each, including beer and wine, salad, poached salmon, and dessert.

After lunch, we went up to the room, washed our clothes, and took a short nap. Later we headed out for a walk around town. We ran into Mike, who was with a Japanese woman who was taking a bus tour along the Camino. Mike spoke some Japanese, so the two of them were engaged in a conversation.

We did some shopping for bread, Ruffles, olives, apples, etc. We were getting pretty comfortable buying our groceries. We had a couple of beers, checked the trail out of town, and headed to the room. Our room had a TV, so we watched the news in Spanish, mostly for the weather forecast, which was for more rain. Not good news.

Today we covered about 13.5 miles in 5.5 hours. Tomorrow we head to Viana, about 12 miles away. We are both hoping our feet hold up and that the rain stays away.

Red or white-Fuente del Vino

View of Villamayor de Monjardin from the old trail

Along the trail before Luquin

Camino traffic jam

CHAPTER 11

September 3, 2003-Wednesday-Day 8
Los Arcos to Viana

12 Miles

GOOD night's sleep. The main Los Arcos church was just outside our room, so the bells woke us up. We have found that in Spain the church bells ring at least every hour, sometimes every fifteen minutes. If your room is near the village church, get ready to hear the bells ringing at all hours.

We were up and away at 7:00 a.m. It was cloudy and cold, and we could see lightning in the distance and hear thunder. It didn't look like we were going to dodge the weather today.

The first couple of miles out of Los Arcos were on a good trail that was next to the main highway. The distant thunderstorms seemed to be moving closer and closer. Just before we reached Sansol, the bottom fell out. We stopped and put on our rain gear. When we reached Sansol, we looked for an open café or bar with no luck. It was still too early. We did make a short stop at a little park in the center of the village. We tried to hide under the overhang of a building for a little shelter. Buddy and Estelle showed up just as we were taking off.

The trail out of Sansol was very muddy and running with water. It dropped down to a creek bed, then climbed up to the village of Torres del Rio. We were not holding out much hope, but we were still looking for a café to get some hot coffee and something to eat. Just when we had given up hope, we found a great bar/café, and better yet, it was open. We went inside where it was warm and out of the rain. The place was very clean and nice. They had a lot of Templar paraphernalia and memorabilia. They also sold maps, pins, etc. We had hot coffee and rolls. This was a great break out of the rain and cold. Buddy and Estelle also made this stop just as we were leaving.

We couldn't stay forever, so we headed out into the rain and hit the trail. As soon as we left Torres del Rio, the trail turned to muck. The soil in this area was mostly clay that, when wet, turned to a slippery, sticky gumbo. This really made for hard walking. We had to watch every step to keep from falling on our butts. Making matters worse, there were a lot of hard uphill climbs with corresponding downhills.

There was nothing between Torres del Rio and Viana, so we had no choice but to keep going. The closer we got to Viana, the harder the rain fell. The mud stuck to our boots like glue, building up with every step. Every hundred feet or so, we had to stop and kick our boots against a rock to knock off the build-up of mud. The mud made our boots weigh about a ton. Every time we went up or down, we would slip and slide.

The last couple of miles were along the road, which made the going a little easier. If we had given it more thought, it might have been a good idea to stay on the road the entire way.

Just when we would get our boots clean from walking on the pavement, the trail would go back off the road into the mud. When we were on the road, we really had to watch out for the cars and trucks. I don't know which was worse. The only good thing about the rain is that it took our minds off our sore feet.

The last part of the trail into Viana went through back alleys with more and more mud. By the time we reached the pavement in town, our boots were soaking wet and covered with mud.

Viana, like many villages and towns in Spain, is built high on a hill, so when you reach your destination, you still have one more good uphill. It continued to rain hard as we made our way to the center of town. We arrived about 1:00 p.m.

We ran into Mike at the main plaza. He said that he had a room in the hostel. We went to a bar that was the check-in place for the hostel and were told that they were full. There were no other hotels or hostels in town. This was not good news because we were cold, wet, and tired of being in the rain. There was a lot of construction going on in Viana. Maybe that was why everything was full. The *albergues* were full, but they would make room; however we were not really anxious to sleep on the floor.

The bar owner gave us the name and address of a woman down the street who sometimes rented rooms to pilgrims. We decided to give it a try. At this point, we had nothing to lose.

We walked down to #23 with Mike as our interpreter. The woman who owned the house answered the door. She and Mike talked in Spanish. She explained that most of her rooms were reserved. After some more conversation, however, she agreed to rent us a small room that had a bathroom down the hall. We were so happy to get out of the rain that we really didn't care that much, so we told her that we would take the room. She ushered us into the house and up to the third floor. We were concerned because our boots were still wet and muddy, but she wouldn't hear anything about that and took us to the room. The room was an interior room with a window out to the stairwell. Small, fairly clean, bathroom right next to our room. The cost was 15 euros each.

We took hot showers and got our clothes washed. As usual we were starved, so we met Mike at the bar to get something to eat. The place was crowded and warm, and the food looked good. We had the Pilgrim's Menu, six euros each. Diddo and I had salad and fried fish with french fries. For dessert Diddo had flan, and I had ice cream. Mike had lentil soup, lamb, and ice cream. The food was great. We felt much better with a full stomach.

We wandered around a little, had some beers, then coffee. We went to the church/*albergue* to get our credentials stamped, then just walked around town.

Mike and a Japanese man we ran into earlier were talking about taking a bus the next day to get out of the rain. Diddo and I had talked about taking a bus, but we had decided to give it a few more days. We both really wanted to walk the entire Camino, but the rain was getting old.

We decided to do a short day tomorrow into Logrono, which is only about seven miles away. If the rain continued, we might be in for a couple of short days. Both of us wanted to keep going and make progress every day. We felt that a short day was better than stopping in one place.

We also talked about staying on the road when it is raining. Mike took the road route from Los Arcos to Viana. He made very good time and avoided the mud. You really just have to pay attention to the traffic.

Approaching Sansol

Long climb before Viana

Street in Viana

Main plaza in Viana

CHAPTER 12

September 4, 2003-Thursday-Day 9
Viana to Logrono

5.5 Miles

DIDN'T sleep very well. The house we were in was very old, and the floors were not very level. I kept getting this feeling that I would roll out of bed if I didn't hold on. There was also a lot of noise during the night, other guests coming and going. It rained so hard all night that it kept waking us up. As we were getting ready, we were not looking forward to going outside into the torrent.

At 8:00 a.m. we were ready to go. We went downstairs to the front door. The rain was so loud we hesitated to go outside. The Japanese man was staying in a small room by the front door. He came out to talk to us. He said that he was going to wait until noon to see if it stopped raining. If not, he was going to take the bus to Logrono. We said goodbye, opened the door, and stepped outside. It was still dark, raining very hard, and cold. Water was running in the street, which was not a good sign. We took off downhill, the same direction as the water. As we got closer to the bottom of the hill, the flooding became worse.

The pavement ended, and we were back in the mud. Luckily, the trail was fairly level. The trail went through bottom-type farmland. Any low points in the trail were filled with water and more mud. Our boots were soaked through within the first hour. We were both starting to have second thoughts about not taking a cab or bus into Logrono. There was thunder and lightning all around us.

We continued on until we saw an alternate trail that led to the road. We decided that the road might be better than the ankle-deep mud we were sloshing through. We reached the road and continued on. The traffic was heavy, with lots of trucks, so we had to really pay attention.

Just before reaching Logrono, we left Navarra and entered Spain's wine country, La Rioja. Although La Rioja is the smallest providence in Spain, it has been a major producer of wine since Roman times. As we walked through La Rioja for the next few days, we were always in or around vineyards that seemed to go on forever.

We didn't see many other pilgrims. Either they hunkered down in Viana or took the bus. The trail gets a little confusing on the outskirts of Logrono. It went under a freeway exchange, then through vineyards. This section of the trail was flooded and very muddy. We finally reached a paved section that went the rest of the way into Logrono.

After going through the outskirts of Logrono, we came to a long bridge over the Rio Ebro. We crossed the bridge and found the street that led to the *albergue*. We had the name of a hotel, but we thought that we would check-in at the *albergue* and get our credentials stamped before looking for a room.

The rain was coming down in buckets when we reached the *albergue*. We tried the door but found that it was locked. A man came to the door and opened it a few inches. He kept it open long enough to tell us and a couple of other pilgrims, that they were closed and that they would open at 3:00 p.m. After this brief statement, he slammed the door shut. Not a very warm and friendly welcome for people standing out in the rain.

We were soaked through and through. Our waterproof jackets were even wet inside. The rain was so heavy that I think the water seeped in around the neck and cuffs.

We continued through the old town into the very busy streets of the main city. We stopped at a hotel listed in our guidebook but found it was closed for remodeling. We walked around in frustration for a few minutes until we saw a NH Hotel across the street. It looked expensive, but at this point we didn't care. We headed over to the NH and walked into the very fancy lobby. The desk clerk looked at us with some suspicion. We didn't blame him. I asked if they had a double room, to which he gave an affirmative reply; 114 euros a night. We took it without hesitation. The desk clerk seemed to relax a little when I pulled out the American Express Platinum Card.

We headed to our room, our boots sloshing against the marbled floor. The room was, to say the least, very nice. As soon as we got inside, we stripped off our wet clothes and took long, hot showers. Worth every euro!

We washed our clothes and got the mud off our boots. Mike had told us yesterday that a good way to dry boots is to pack them with newspaper. The idea is that the newspaper draws the water out of the boots. We decided to give it a try. I went to the lobby area and grabbed several newspapers. We packed our boots with the newspaper, hoping for the best. About a hour later, we took the soaking wet newspapers out and re-packed the boots. Believe it or not, it worked great. A few hours later, we had dry boots.

After getting warm and dry, we headed out to get something to eat. The assistant desk clerk spoke English and told us where there was a nearby Internet café. We wanted to send some e-mail and check the weather forecast. We were getting really close to taking a bus down the road if things didn't improve. We found the Internet café with no trouble and sent e-mail to our daughters, family, and friends. We checked the forecast. It called for more rain tomorrow.

We walked around and found an Irish pub that looked like a good place for lunch. We had the Menu of the Day that included salad, beefsteak with french fries, with an apple for dessert. We also had a couple of beers. The bill came to nine euros each. A good hot meal on a cold rainy day helped to lift our sprits a little.

We did some shopping and purchased a couple more ponchos, just to have as extras because it looked like we might need them. We picked up some bread, chorizo, chocolate bars, Vaseline, and more newspapers to pack our boots.

Later we stopped at a tapas bar. The tapas bars offer a wide variety of snacks or appetizers, such as stuffed mushrooms, small sandwiches, olives, etc. They are a good choice if you are in-between meal times. We had a couple of beers and some tapas.

Back at the room we re-packed the boots and talked about tomorrow. We decided to see what the weather was like in the morning. Neither of us wanted to take the bus. It felt like we would be admitting defeat. We decided to do another short day tomorrow to Navarette, about seven or eight miles.

Neither one of us was looking forward to many more soaking wet days, but we were both hoping for the best.

Today we covered about seven miles in three hours. Hoping for a good night's sleep and better weather.

CHAPTER 13

September 5, 2003-Friday-Day 10
Logrono to Navarrete

8 Miles

IT rained most of the night but ceased shortly before we hit the trail. As we walked through the busy morning streets of Logrono, we kept a close eye on the heavens. We didn't take off until 8:00 a.m. We were in no big hurry because we were planning a short day.

The Camino goes through downtown Logrono. We had to really keep on our toes to find the yellow arrows. On the outskirts of town, there is a dedicated paved trail that goes through a park/lake area. The guidebook lists a coffee shop by the lake, but it was still closed. We were really looking forward to a hot cup of coffee.

On the outskirts of the park, a man had set up a table and was serving coffee and cookies to pilgrims. We stopped there to take a short break. We ran into the Japanese fellow. He said that he took the bus from Viana to Logrono. We also ran into Nadia from Brazil. We had not seen her since Cizur Menor. She said she had a layover in Logrono because she had a problem with her feet and had to see a doctor. She felt better, but she didn't know how far she would be able to go.

The trail left the valley where Logrono is located and after a steady but not killer climb, went over a ridge. It warmed up to the point that we shed our jackets.

After reaching the top of the ridge, the trail paralleled the freeway. There were hundreds of small, hand-made crosses in the freeway fence. They went on for about a quarter of a mile. We never did find out the meaning behind the crosses. We went over the ridge into the next valley. The town of Navarrete, our destination for the day, was visible in front of us. After dropping down into the valley, we crossed over the freeway on a footbridge into Navarrete. Before entering the town, we passed by the ruins of the Hospital de San Juan de Acre, a hospice dating back to the 12th Century. We reached the *albergue* three hours after leaving our hotel in Logrono. The total distance today was about eight miles.

We stopped at the Los Arcos bar, located next to the *albergue*. We had coffee, rolls, and a bag of Ruffles. We inquired at the bar and were given directions to the San Camilo Hotel. It was located on the outskirts of town.

When we got to the hotel, we didn't think that we were in the right place. The San Camilo must have been built as a resort or luxury spa. It is an older hotel, but very nice and well maintained. The grounds were beautiful.

We walked through the entrance into the parking lot. There were no vehicles parked in the lot. We wondered if the hotel was even open. We found the main entrance and went to the desk. They were open and had a room. Actually, it looked like they had lots of rooms. We checked in: 69 euros, with a ten percent pilgrim's discount. We headed to our room, which was very nice, clean, and had the greatest shower in the world. It had about ten showerheads that hit you all over. We took showers, washed our clothes, and headed back into town to have our credentials stamped and get something to eat. It still looked like we were the only people checked into the hotel.

In town we took what we thought was a shortcut and got lost for about ten minutes. We backtracked to the *albergue*, waited in line for a few minutes, and got our credentials stamped. The *albergue* was filled past capacity. This would prove to be the case in almost every *albergue* on the Camino.

We found a bar, the Café Molina that was serving lunch. We had the Menu del Dia: paella con carne, pork filets with french fries, and chocolate mousse for dessert. With bottled water the cost was seven and a half euros each.

We went back to the Los Arcos bar, had a couple of beers, and watched pilgrims arrive at the *albergue*. The clouds had cleared away, and it turned out to be a warm, sunny day.

The last couple of rainy days must have tired us out a little. We headed back to the room to relax. I was glad to see when we returned to the hotel that other guests had checked in. I was beginning to think that there was something strange about the place. I kept expecting to see Jack Nicholson coming around a corner with an axe in his hand yelling, "Here's Johnny!"

We are looking at about nine miles tomorrow to Najera; hope this nice weather holds!

Important note: The Camino is a physical and mental challenge. One day you are sloshing through ankle-deep mud, soaking wet. You are tired, it's raining, and it is freezing cold. You start talking about taking a bus to get out of the area. You stay in an *albergue* or a noisy, dirty, smelly room. The next day, you have great weather, great hiking, a good hotel room, good food, and you are completely recharged.

You have to try not to worry about what is up ahead and just deal with today and maybe your plans for tomorrow. You also should not push yourself too much. Several people who started with us and who were going for high mileage every day, were starting to have physical problems.

It is hard to deal with several heavy rain days in a row, but once you get dried out, everything seems OK. You need to focus on what is right in front of you. Always move ahead. If you need a rest, do one or two short-mileage days.

View back toward Logrono

Camino into Navarrete

San Camilo Hotel

View of Navarrete

CHAPTER 14

September 6, 2003-Saturday-Day 11
Navarrete to Najera

10.5 Miles

DIDN'T sleep that well last night. I kept thinking about all of the things that have happened to us since we started this adventure.

We were planning another short day, so we didn't take off until 8:10 a.m. Before we left, we had the hotel desk clerk make a reservation for us at the Hotel San Fernando in Najera. Both hotels are owned by the same company.

The weather was cool and overcast, but no rain. Fairly flat walking with some up and downs, but nothing bad. The entire day we traveled through mile after mile of vineyards.

We stopped at 9:50 a.m. on the side of the trail and, using rocks for our table and chairs, ate a snack of bread, chorizo and cheese. We started on the only real uphill of the day, heading to a mesa, where the trail leveled out for a couple of miles.

We dropped down off the mesa into the next valley where Najera is located. Red clay soil-glad it is not raining, or this would be a real mess. On the outskirts of Najera, we walked through an industrial area where the trail became confusing at times.

On a factory wall just outside of Najera is a hand-painted Pilgrim's Poem. It is in Spanish, but roughly translated it reads:

Dust, mud, sun and rain
Camino de Santiago
Thousands of pilgrims
And more than a thousand years.

Pilgrim, who calls you?
What hidden force attracts you?
Not the fields of stars
Not the grand cathedrals.

It isn't the brave Navarra,
Nor the wine of the Riojanos,
Nor the Galician seafood
Nor the Castillian fields.

Pilgrim, who calls you?
What hidden force attracts you?
Not the people of the Camino
Nor the rural customs.

It isn't the history or culture
Nor the hen of La Calzada
Nor the Palace of Gaudi
Nor the Castle of Ponferrada.

I see it all in passing
It is a pleasure to see it all
Plus the voice that calls me
I feel much deeper.

The force that pushes me
The force that attracts me
I can't even explain
Only the One above knows!

The poem is signed with the initials E.G.B. It is a beautiful poem with a very powerful message and a powerful question.

Najera was a very busy town. Lots of hustle and bustle, which always threw us a little after being out on the trail. We arrived in Najera at 12:10 p.m., about four hours to cover ten or so miles. We walked around until we located the Hotel San Fernando. Very nice hotel, but we had a very small room, with a very small bed.

Following our usual routine, we took showers and washed our clothes. We headed down to the hotel restaurant for lunch. The Menu del Dia consisted of calamari, lamb cutlets with french fries, ice cream for dessert, and a bottle of wine and water. Ten and a half euros each.

We walked over the bridge to the main part of town and found the *albergue.* We had our credentials stamped and hung around to see who showed up.

A tall young man, Igor, 22 years old from Salt Lake City, arrived a short time later. He heard us speaking English, so he came over and introduced himself. He said that he had found himself in a job he didn't really like and in a relationship that he wasn't sure of. After reading an article about the Camino a month ago, he decided to make the trip. He said that he had never done anything this adventurous before and that he was not a hiker. He came to Spain on a non-rev (employee/no cost) ticket with very little money, but with a little help from his parents in the form of a money gram, he was doing OK.

This young man seemed to be very happy with his quest and seemed to be covering a lot of ground really fast. When he tried to check into the *albergue*, he, along with several other pilgrims, was informed that it was overcrowded and not taking any more people. Igor picked up his pack and headed out for the next *albergue* in Azofra, almost three miles away. Three miles doesn't seem like a great distance, but at the end of a long day of hiking, it can seem forever.

We also met Jessica from New York and her father from Toronto. Jessica did the Camino six years ago. Her dad was doing it this year. She had come this far with her dad to get him started. Jessica was going to catch a bus to Madrid in the morning, then fly home. We talked about how overcrowded the *albergue*s were, and how few Americans seemed to be on the Camino.

We walked around town, bought postcards and stamps, and looked for a bookstore with English language books with no luck. We stopped at a tapas bar, had beers and stuffed mushrooms that were great. I also picked up four bags of Ruffles potato chips, my weakness on the Camino.

We did our usual routine of walking the first half-mile or so on the trail out of town. We returned to the room and found that the TV had CNN in English. It seemed like a luxury to catch up on the news.

My knee is finally healing, and our feet don't seem to hurt as much. We plan on doing 12 to 13 miles tomorrow from Najera to Santo Domingo de Calzada. Forecast is for rain. We're hoping the good weather holds.

Roldan's Podium between Ventosa and Najera

Pilgrim's poem outside of Najera

Najera

CHAPTER 15

September 7, 2003-Sunday-Day 12
Najera to Santo Domingo

13 Miles

THE bed proved to be too small for us to get a good night's sleep, but it was still better than a floor at the *albergue*. We took off at 7:30 a.m. It was cloudy and looked like rain. Long uphill climb out of Najera. Red clay soil and grapevines as far as you could see.

About sunup, it started to rain. We made a short stop and put on our rain gear. It was raining hard by the time we reached Azofra. There was only one bar in Azofra, and every pilgrim seemed to be crowded inside the place. We had to stand in line to order. There were only two people working in the bar, and, of course, they make every cup of coffee one at a time. I learned a good lesson here. The guy next to me ordered three cups of coffee; I ordered two. The waiter gave an order for five cups of coffee to the owner, who was making the coffee. The owner served the five cups onto the counter. I asked him how much I owed. He seemed confused because in Spain you pay as you leave. You just tell them what you had, kind of an honor system. I hadn't figured this out yet, so I asked again, "How much for the coffee?" The owner replied, "Five euros." I paid, took the coffee to our table, and complained to Diddo that the coffee was expensive. After we left the bar, it dawned on me that the owner charged me for all five coffees. My mistake, but at least I learned how things work.

The rain had lightened up, but it was still cold and windy. The rain would come and go the rest of the day. The ponchos were getting a workout going on and off. Fairly easy walking until a long, hard climb up to Ciruena. Just before the village, we walked by a golf course and country club. There was a lot of construction in this area with several detours.

After Ciruena, we decided to take a break. We were on a mesa with nothing around so, again, rocks were our table and chairs. We had some chorizo that we had bought in a small *supermercado* in Logrono, but it wasn't very good. After that we only purchased chorizo in a *carniceria*.

We took off again, and when we reached the edge of the mesa, Santo Domingo was visible a short distance away. We did not realize that we were so close. We continued on a long downhill off the mesa. We kept hearing gunshots. After looking around, we noticed several bird hunters with dogs, working the freshly cut fields in the area. We learned later that the hunting season had just opened.

We arrived in Santo Domingo at about 1:30 p.m. It had taken about five and a half hours to cover 13 miles. We walked down the street leading to the old town section. We were looking for the El Corregidor Hotel that was listed in our guidebook. It turned out to be a very nice, older hotel. Our room was 89 euros.

We did our usual clean-up job and went down to the hotel restaurant. We had the Menu del Dia: paella, leg of lamb, and ice cream. The meal was 12 euros each, including wine.

We walked around town taking in the sights. Almost everything was closed because it was Sunday. The *albergue* was already way overcrowded. They were putting mats on the floor to handle the overflow. We went into the lobby of the Parador, a very luxurious hotel run by the Spanish government. It was very impressive.

We took the trail out of town for about a half mile. We walked around until we found a pastry shop open where we bought some bread. We had a couple of beers, than returned to the room to watch the weather report in Spanish and our favorite Spanish soap opera. Hoping for a good night's sleep and good weather tomorrow.

Santo Domingo

CHAPTER 16

September 8, 2003-Monday-Day 13
Santo Domingo to Belorado

15 Miles

WE headed out at 7:00 a.m. It was cold and very windy. When we reached the outskirts of town, we had to stop and put on our jackets. About a quarter mile out of town, there was a fork in the trail. There were no markers that we could see, so we continued on the path that followed the road. This didn't look like the route shown on the map. We heard someone calling out to us. We stopped, turned around, and saw a man waving us back to where the trail went off to the right. We walked back to that location. He told us in English that we were going the wrong way. We all introduced ourselves. Bill, the man who had called us back, was a retired travel agent from North Toronto, Canada.

We all took off, this time on the right trail. Bill was doing the Camino by himself. He said that he was anxious to complete the Camino because he and his wife had just been given custody of their grandson, and they were looking forward to the experience of being parents again. We all walked together for most of the day.

Today, between Santo Domingo and Belorado, we left La Rioja and entered Castilla y Leon. Castilla y Leon is by far the largest autonomous region in Spain. Castilla y Leon is made up of nine separate provinces, three of which we would walk through on the Camino. We were still in wine country, but would soon enter the Meseta.

After a flat stretch, the trail started a long uphill climb. The wind was getting stronger as the day went on, and clouds were forming all around us. The trail was great, and generally went alongside of the main road. We went through several small villages, but found no open bars or cafes. The strong wind was really giving the mountain bikers on the Camino a tough time.

Talking with Bill seemed to make the miles go by faster. About three miles before Belorado, Bill said he was going to take a break. We had a good rhythm going, so we continued on. It was also getting windier, colder, and looking more and more like rain. After reaching the high point of today's trail, we started on a long downhill into Belorado. We reached Belorado about noon.

Belorado is in a beautiful valley, but the town itself seemed to be neglected. Belorado is a highway town, so it is long and narrow. After reaching town, we had to walk all the way through to get to the hotel we were looking for. The streets were full of trash and rubbish. It looked like Belorado had seen better days, but maybe we just arrived on a bad day.

We passed the *albergue* just after arriving, and it was already filling up. After the long walk through town, we found the Belorado Hotel. We went into the bar and contacted the manager, who we believe was one of two brothers who owned the hotel. We started referring to them as the "Belorado Brothers." We asked about a double room with bath. Belorado Brother #1 got the ledger and studied it for about five minutes before telling us that he did have a room. It turned out to be the last one, because a couple came in after us and were turned away. B.B. #1 said that the room would be ready in about 30 minutes. We left our gear in the office and went out in search of supplies.

We found a *supermercado* and bought cheese, chorizo, fruit, candy bars, Ruffles, and toothpaste. We returned, had a beer in the bar, and then went to our room. The room was low-end and was located just above the entrance to the bar, on the main road.

We took showers and washed our clothes, then headed downstairs to the hotel restaurant. B.B.#2 seemed to be running the restaurant. After being seated, we asked him about the Menu del Dia. He seemed frustrated with us and just started bringing us food. I don't think that he wanted to deal with us, and the menu. I had bean and sausage soup, beefsteak with french fries, and ice cream. We paid for the room and meals all together, 54 euros.

After lunch, we headed back to the other side of town to the *albergue* and had our credentials stamped. We ran into Bill on the way and agreed to meet him later at the plaza for a beer.

The main plaza looked like it would be a great place if it were cleaned up.

Bill and some of the other pilgrims complained that the manager at the *albergue* was not a very nice guy. They said that he was very short-tempered with the pilgrims and demanded that everyone speak Spanish.

We headed back to the hotel, where we met Helen and Jim. They were doing the Camino in sections each year. Jim did the entire Camino five years ago. Jim said that it was great back then because there were so few pilgrims. Today they had hiked from Belorado to San Juan de Ortega. They had returned to Belorado in a cab. Their plan was to take a cab back to San Juan de Ortega tomorrow and continue on foot from there.

The weather continued to deteriorate, but still no rain. We were planning a short day tomorrow to Villafranca de Montes de Oca, about seven miles. It is the only place to stay before going over the mountains, other than San Juan de Ortega. San Juan de Ortega only has an *albergue* that is always overcrowded and can be very cold. We were both concerned about the weather because we were going over the mountains.

CHAPTER 17

September 9, 2003-Tuesday-Day 14
Belorado to Villafranca de Montes de Oca

7.5 Miles

SLEPT OK, lots of road noise and noise from the bar during the night. It was very cold and cloudy, but no rain so far. Nice trail, generally uphill, heading into the mountains. We were going to stop for the night at Villafranca de Montes de Oca, which is only seven or so miles from Belorado. The weather looked so bad that we didn't want to chance getting hit at the higher altitudes.

I was beginning to feel we were not doing enough mileage each day. We had been getting progressively stronger. Our feet didn't hurt as much at the end of the day, and we were confident with life on the trail. I had been thinking that we should try a couple of long days, 18 miles or so, to see how we would do. I talked to Diddo about this, and she told me that she had been thinking the same thing. Based on our discussion, we decided to go from Villafranca de Montes de Oca all the way to Burgos the following day. This is a distance of about 19 miles, over the mountains. We both knew that this would be a real challenge, but we were looking forward to it

We reached Villafranca de Montes de Oca around 11:00 a.m. Villafranca de Montes de Oca is in a wooded valley in the foothills. It is a highway town with a truck stop and not a lot else. There were rooms for rent upstairs at the truck stop, and there is also an *albergue*. We had been told in Santo Domingo that the *albergue* was closed, so we went directly to the truck stop to get a room. (It turned out that the *albergue* was open, and had plenty of room.)

We checked in at the bar and got a room with a shared bathroom down the hall, for 30 euros.

The weather had deteriorated. It was very windy outside, with heavy clouds, and it looked like rain.

We did our laundry, and took showers before too many other people showed up to rent rooms. We went downstairs to the truck-stop restaurant and had the Menu del Dia. Eight and a half euros each for rice salad, salmon (not a filet, lots of bones) french fries, and ice cream for dessert. OK, but nothing special.

We are both excited about the long haul tomorrow, hoping the weather clears.

CHAPTER 18

September 10, 2003-Wednesday-Day 15
Villafranca de Montes de Oca to Burgos (Villafria)

19 Miles

SLEPT OK, lots of road noise, heavy trucks on the highway. It got so cold during the night that I had to use my sleeping bag to supplement the bed covers.

We were up early and on the trail by 6:30 a.m. It was very dark and cold, but clear as a bell, not a cloud in sight. The trail was straight up out of Villafranca de Montes de Oca. It was so dark that we couldn't see a thing without our headlamps. The trail was not well marked, so we had to take our time checking for the yellow arrows. This made the going slow, but we didn't want to take the wrong trail. The only other pilgrims on the trail at this time in the morning were three German men who were in front of us.

As daylight started to break, we reached the top of the climb, a high mesa with beautiful pine forest and a great trail. We had been so worried about rain, but it turned out to be a beautiful, sunny day. We couldn't ask for anything better for our first attempt at a high-mileage day.

We reached San Juan de Ortega about nine o'clock. Beautiful setting, but it looks like it gets pretty cold after sundown. We stopped at a café next to the church and *albergue* for a hot cup of coffee and donuts. The German men were there also taking a break. Two women showed up just as we were leaving. We exchanged greetings in English and talked to them for just a minute.

The trail out of San Juan de Ortega was fairly flat but very rocky. We went through the village of Ages, then into Atapuerca. Atapuerca is the site of prehistoric ruins that are believed to be some of the oldest in Europe. The German men were taking a break at a bar in Atapuerca, so we joined them. We had coffee and some hot, freshly made *tortillas* with lots of potatoes, which were very good. A Japanese woman showed up who seemed to know the Germans. They all took off together.

For no particular reason, I wanted to beat the Germans into Burgos. We had been behind them all day, and my competitive spirit had been aroused. There is a long, steep, and very rocky climb out of Atapuerca to a high ridge overlooking the valley where Burgos is located. We struggled past the Germans as we all climbed up to the ridge. When we were passing them, all of us gasping for breath, I asked them if they wanted to race. We all got a good laugh out of this, which made the climb a little easier. We did manage to stay in front of them the rest of the way into Burgos.

When we did reach the top of the ridge, we were rewarded with a great view. Burgos is the start of the Meseta, "The Plains of Spain," so from this ridge we could see forever.

From this high mesa, it was a very long, knee-killing downhill to the valley below. We took a short break in the village of Cardenuela de Rio Pico and then continued on. The trail went along next to the road all the way to Villafria, a suburb of Burgos.

We reached Villafria at 2:30 p.m. Eight hours to cover about 19 miles over the mountains. We were tired but felt good about the long day.

The Buenos Aires Hotel listed in our guidebook is on the main road into Burgos. The place is old, but very well maintained. We got a nice room for 40 euros.

Because of the time, we went right to lunch at the hotel restaurant. The Menu del Dia was 10 euros each. I had hot barley soup, beefsteak with fries, and ice cream. The meal, along with a couple of beers, really hit the spot.

We headed to the room, took showers, and did our wash. We kicked back for a while, then went out to see what Villafria was all about. Villafria is an industrial area, and there was not really too much to see. We checked the trail markings for the next day and then headed back to the hotel.

On the way back, we stopped at a gas station that had a small store to pick up some bottled water and candy bars. We placed the items on the counter and waited for the clerk. He was outside at the gas pumps helping customers. When he came inside to ring up the gas customers, he told us he would be right with us. He seemed somewhat upset. We told him that we were not in a hurry. He rushed back outside, then back into the office to ring up the next customer. He told us the same thing and seemed even more upset. We couldn't figure out why he was so irritated. We weren't in any hurry, and we weren't putting any pressure on the guy. On his third trip, he rang up our stuff and apologized for the delay. We told him that it was no problem and left shaking our heads.

Before going back to the room, we went to the hotel bar and ordered a couple of beers. The two women we had seen briefly in Villafranca de Montes de Oca and San Juan de Ortega came into the bar. They said hello to us, so we all introduced ourselves. Teresa and Heather were both Canadians. They were doing the Camino on a very tight schedule. They started two days after us and had to be in Santiago by the 28th of September. We all sat around drinking beer and telling Camino war stories. We all had a good time just sitting around and talking. They had great attitudes and, like us, were having a good time on the Camino. We enjoyed their company that evening and for several days to come.

Our plan was to get an early start in the morning and continue with our high-mileage strategy. We both felt good after the long walk and were looking forward to the next day's trek. I think that today was our best hiking day so far. Everything seemed perfect. We both felt good, the weather was great (for the first time since we started), and the trail was beautiful.

Ahead of us is the Meseta. This will be like marching across Kansas or Nebraska: flat, rolling hills, wheat fields, very few trees, little or no shade, long distances between villages. It looked like we were in for warmer, maybe even hot, weather. We were both looking forward to the change.

Early morning out of Villafranca de Montes de Oca

Trail between Villafranca and San Juan de Ortega

Church and albergue at San Juan de Ortega

Camino out of San Juan de Ortega

Downhill into Ages

Medieval bridge Puente de San Juan

Atapuerca-one of the earliest settlements in Europe

View from high ridge toward Burgos

CHAPTER 19

September 11, 2003-Thursday-Day 16
Burgos (Villafria) to Hornillos

17 Miles

WEIRD feeling being here on 9-11. The attack two years ago is still so crystal clear in our minds. Others we encountered on the Camino today, from many countries, had the same feeling.

We were on the trail, or should I say sidewalk, at 6:30 a.m. It seemed to take forever to get through Burgos, a very large and busy city. After being out in the rural areas for so long, going through the large city seemed strange because of the traffic, congestion, and all of the people.

When we reached the center of town, we found a cafe that had just opened. We made our morning stop for coffee and *tortilla*s. Both were fresh and tasted great. The Camino path goes by the Burgos Cathedral, a very impressive sight.

We stopped at the *albergue* to have our credentials stamped. It is located in a large city park on the west side of Burgos. The Burgos *albergue* looked like a nice clean place. We took a short break there.

The last time we had seen Mike, back in Viana, he said that he would leave us a note at the *albergue* in Burgos. I checked for a note on the bulletin board but didn't find anything. I don't know if Mike took a bus further on or dropped out. We did not see him again.

It took us almost three hours to reach the outskirts of Burgos. We were back in the countryside, under clear sunny skies. The trail went by what looked like a prison, then through a stand of trees, planted in perfect rows. We would see these rows of trees all across the Meseta. There must be some plan to reforest the region. The trail went along a river for a short distance, then under the freeway. About two miles later we reached the village of Tardajos. It had warmed up quite a bit. We stopped for a break at a small park in the center of town. I went across the street to a bar and got a ham and cheese *bocadillo*. We sat in a little park and ate.

The trail out of Tardajos goes along the road. We noticed many nuns walking along the road. They were from a convent in the village of Rabe de las Calzadas, the next village we went through. After Rabe de las Calzadas, the trail turned into a dirt road and started a long hard uphill to a high mesa. No shade anywhere. The top of the mesa seemed to get farther away with each step. Just when the going got really tough, we saw a shelter just off the trail. We headed over there and found a covered fountain with tables, cold water and shade. It felt so good to take our packs off and take a break in the shade. I soaked my hat and then splashed the cold, clear water from the fountain on my face. It doesn't get much better than that. Sitting here writing this, it seems like such a simple thing, but there, being out of the sun, the shade, the cold water, it was just like heaven!

While we were enjoying the break, an older man accompanied by two young women walked over to the shelter. We introduced ourselves. Lester, a dentist from Canada, was trying the Camino for the second time. His first attempt was in September of 2001. He hurt his knee on the first day out of St. Jean. When 9-11 hit, he was in Burgos. He had been forced to stop there because of his knee injury. This year, he flew into Burgos, and planned to walk the Camino for two weeks. One of the young women had just graduated from William and Mary College. She wanted to do the Camino before she started her career. All three had started in Burgos today.

It was still a long haul to the top of the mesa, but the break made it a lot easier. After a short level walk across the mesa, there was a steep downhill into Hornillos. Even though we reached Hornillos early, the *albergue* was already full. There were no other places to stay in Hornillos or close by. Diddo found the *albergue* manager, who agreed to give us a place-a mattress on the kitchen floor. Not the Ritz, but better than nothing and only four euros each.

More and more pilgrims arrived, including Teresa and Heather, the two Canadians. There were so many pilgrims looking for a place to stay that a townsperson rented out floor space and mats in a building he owned.

We were too late for lunch in the restaurant section of the bar in the village, so we sat in the bar and ordered calamari and a salad. Of course, due to the heat, we also needed a few ice-cold beers. The cost was about 10 euros.

At the rear of the *albergue*, they had an area to wash clothes. We took advantage of the laundry facilities then headed back to our "room," where we organized our gear for an early getaway in the morning.

Later in the evening, we went back to the bar for some more beer, calamari, and boiled chorizo with bread. It really hit the spot, and only cost a total of eight euros. Teresa, Heather, Lester, and the two young women all joined us at the bar. This was always a nice part of the day, sitting around with other pilgrims, trading stories, and relaxing.

When we got back to the *albergue*, we found a young man from Hungary who had been given a space just at the foot of our mats. Close quarters, but everyone needed shelter.

After lights out, a major dogfight erupted just outside our window. We all tried to quiet the dogs but were unsuccessful. Finally, the old *albergue* manager went out and ran the dogs off. I knew I would not get much sleep tonight.

Today we covered about 17 miles in 7.5 hours. My feet hurt, but everything else was OK. Tomorrow should be about 12 miles with one major climb right out of the gate. It looked like we were in for warm sunny weather.

The *albergue* manager here is an interesting guy. He is 78 years old. He was a farmer from Hornillos. He did the Camino many years ago. He is now retired. He could not understand why I was retired at such a young age. I explained why.

Weird to be here on 9-11

Cathedral in Burgos

Cathedral

View back toward Rabe from rest stop

Long downhill into Hornillos

Hornillos albergue

Kitchen floor lodging

Church in Hornillos

CHAPTER 20

September 12, 2003-Friday-Day 17
Hornillos to Castrojeriz

13.5 Miles

WHAT a night. Between the dogfight, the water heater going on and off, and the warden checking in people in the middle of the night, we got about one hour of sleep. We had no choice but to get up early since people were in the kitchen preparing coffee and breakfast. After a quick cup of coffee, we hit the trail.

There is a long, steep climb right out of Hornillos. The weather was clear and cool, so we set a fast pace. We reached the top of the mesa just as the sun came up.

Last night, a young pilgrim came to the *albergue* looking for a space. He continued on due to the overcrowded conditions. I noticed that he was carrying a tent, which is a rare sight on the Camino. We passed his campsite on top of the mesa just as he was waking up. That didn't look like too bad of a deal. At least he didn't have to contend with all of the action at the *albergue*.

As we continued on, we went by an interesting *albergue* at Son Bol. It was small, but appeared to be very neat and clean. The guidebook said that they only have a few beds and not much else. Apparently this place was completely redone in the recent past by a group claiming to be with the Knights Templar.

A short distance later, the trail went downhill off the mesa into the village of Hontanas. We were hungry and ready for some coffee. The only café open did not look all that clean, but it was the only game in town.

The owner's claim to fame is that he can pour wine on his forehead that runs down his nose, then into his mouth. There were several newspaper accounts of this feat lining the wall of the café. Unfortunately, I watched him wash the coffee cups in the dishwater. It didn't look like it had been changed for a very long time.

The trail leaves Hontanas then proceeds down a valley. Fairly flat walking. We noticed thousands of seedling trees planted on the sides of this valley.

About two and a half miles out of Hontanas, we came to the ruins of the monastery and hospice of Arco de San Anton. This was the location of the Antonine Order. One of their symbols is a cross that looks like the letter "T." This symbol is known as "Tau" and seemed to be quite well known. We took a break for a few minutes there. It was a very relaxing place, with a small gift shop and store, along with a private *albergue*.

At this point, we were walking along the road that continued to Castrojeriz. Castrojeriz was visible about two miles away. It got somewhat boring because we could see our destination, and there was not much in between. The trail was very flat, exposed, and went along next to the road. The area around here looks like desert: very little shade and sandy/rocky soil. The weather was also very desert-like, warm and dry.

We arrived in Castrojeriz and started searching for a hotel. We had the names of three good hotels from a tourist pamphlet that we picked up in Santo Domingo. We didn't expect any problem finding a room. We were looking forward to a nice place to make up for last night. After what seemed like a long walk through town, we arrived at the hotel that was our first choice. All of the doors were locked, and a sign said that the hotel was closed for business. No problem, we had the names of the other two hotels in town.

We went to the second hotel/hostel and entered the lobby. It looked like a nice place. There wasn't anyone at the desk, so we dropped our packs and sat down for about ten minutes. We called out for the clerk and walked around looking for someone to assist us, with no luck. I went back outside and found a sign in Spanish that said to check in at the bar down the street. I left Diddo at the hotel and went to the bar. After the usual conversation with the bartender/hotel clerk in English, Spanish, and sign language, I got the message that the hotel and hostel were full. No problem, still one more to go.

We grabbed our gear and started back the way we had come to the location of the third hotel. The door was locked, which we took as a bad sign. We rang the bell, which was answered by a nice woman who advised us that they were full.

Completely dejected, we started back to the main section of town. The thought of spending another night at an overcrowded *albergue* was not appealing, but there didn't appear to be any other choice.

As we were headed in the direction of the *albergue*, we saw a building that had the letter "P" on a sign by the front door. This is the symbol for a *pension*. We thought we would give it a try. We rang the bell and were soon greeted by a man with blond hair. We inquired in Spanish if they had any rooms. The gentleman asked us in English where we were from. We told him, and he introduced himself as Jos. Jos spoke perfect English. Turns out that he and his wife were from Holland. They moved here a couple of years ago after visiting Castrojeriz. They purchased the building and turned it into a *pension*, La Casa de los Holandeses. He invited us in and said that the place had three bedrooms, which shared one bathroom. We noticed that the interior was spotless and decorated nicely. We immediately said that we would take a room. Jos took us upstairs and showed us the three rooms so that we could make our choice. We picked one overlooking the street. All of the rooms were spotless and beautifully decorated. It was more like a very nice bed and breakfast, without the breakfast. Jos took a lot of pride in the place that he and his wife had completely rebuilt. Our room was 30 euros. What a deal!

We went to our room and immediately took showers and washed our clothes before any other guest arrived. Within a few minutes, two French couples arrived and took the other two rooms. We had seen these people on the trail for the last couple of days. Glad we got here when we did.

We learned later from Jos's wife that the bird-hunting season had just opened. All of the rooms in town were filled with people who come from all over Spain to hunt in the area around Castrojeriz.

We were learning the hard way that the closer you get to Santiago, the more crowded the Camino becomes. Already crowded *albergue*s, hostels, and hotels filled up early in the day. Because of this, we decided to make reservations whenever we were able to. Our tourist pamphlet listed a Hotel San Martin in Fromista, our next stop. We asked Jos and his wife the location of the nearest pay telephone. Mrs. Jos immediately took the hotel information, used their telephone, and made a reservation for us. Jos and his wife were nice people and great hosts, the type of folks who make certain days on the Camino stand out.

As usual, we were starved. Jos recommended a bar just across the street. We headed over for a late lunch. When we entered, we found Heather and Teresa. They were eating and having wine and beer. We asked them where they were staying. They replied that they were going on to the *albergue* at Ermita de San Nicolas, another five hard miles, with a huge uphill climb out of Castrojeriz. I thought that they were crazy. It was very hot outside, and it was getting late in the day.

The Ermita de San Nicolas *albergue* is known for serving the pilgrims who stay there an evening meal. There is no power, so everything is done in candlelight. Also, there are only 12 beds, and they do not allow any overflow. If you get there and they are full, you have a problem.

Heather and Teresa finished their drinks, said goodbye, and took off. We ordered the Menu del Dia: meat and potato soup, pork ribs with fries, and ice cream. I was very hungry. The ribs had a lot of fat on them, but I am ashamed to say that I ate everything down to the bone. Diddo said that she wasn't very hungry, so she didn't eat very much.

The bar had a pay Internet computer, so I signed on and sent e-mail to family and friends with updates on our progress. I checked my e-mail and found an e-mail to us from our daughter Deborah. By the time I finished reading it, I had tears in my eyes. Her message touched our hearts, and I think that we were both starting to miss our daughters.

We walked around town and purchased bread, fruit, cookies, potato chips, and candy bars. I also found some pads for the balls of my feet. That is the area where my feet hurt the most, so I thought I would give them a try. It turned out that they did not do any good; in fact, I think they made matters worse. I tossed them out a couple of days later.

Crossing the Meseta is a real challenge. It can be very hot, featureless, dry, and boring. You have to find a rhythm within yourself or you will go crazy. The afternoon heat can really fry you, so we were going to leave early in the morning to try to beat the heat.

Later we went to the bar and had a light snack and a couple of beers. We returned to the room and hit the sack early. We covered about 13.5 miles today in 5 hours. Tomorrow will be 16 miles plus.

San Bol albergue

Downhill into Hontanas

Monastery-Arco de San Anton

Heading into Castrojeriz

La Casa de los Holandeses

CHAPTER 21

September 13, 2003-Saturday-Day 18
Castrojeriz to Fromista

16.5 Miles

GREAT night's sleep. We were on the move by 6:30 a.m. It was very dark outside, so we had to use our headlights all the way through town.

After leaving town, the trail went down to the road, crossed over, and entered a wide river valley. We then started a long, steep, rocky uphill climb. It was at least one mile up to the top of the mesa. We were glad we were doing this in the dark, so we couldn't see how steep the grade was. I don't know how Heather and Teresa did this in the hot sun after drinking beer and wine.

At 7:30 a.m., we reached the top of the mesa. This was the high point of today's trek. The eastern sky was just starting to get light. It was as clear as a bell, stars everywhere, and we could see forever in every direction. It was very dry and cool, and there was a light breeze blowing. I will always remember this morning. We stood there taking a short break after the climb, and everything was just beyond belief. The whole experience; being here in Spain, doing this pilgrimage, life in general, it was one of those times for me when everything just seemed perfect.

We walked the short distance across the mesa, then began a steep downhill into the valley. The sun had just come up, it was still cool, but we could tell it was going to be a hot day. Our plan was to keep going at a good pace and try to reach Fromista early to beat the heat.

We passed the Saint Nicolas *albergue*. It looked like Heather and Teresa had already left. The young man with the tent was camped on the lawn outside of the *albergue*.

We crossed the Rio Pisuerga, then reached the village of Itero de la Vega. There was a tobacco store that served coffee and rolls, so we decided to take our morning break. We had coffee *con leche*, and *magdalanas*. *Magdalanas* are a small cake snack that you can find in almost every store. We always had some in our pack to eat out on the trail. The coffee didn't taste that good, but I didn't give it much thought.

About a mile down the trail, Diddo stopped all of a sudden and said that she felt lightheaded. She took off her jacket, and we took a five-minute break. She had not eaten much yesterday, and I thought that might be the problem. I had a problem also; my stomach was sending me a message that I better find a restroom real quick. Unfortunately for me, there were no restrooms for miles. We were in the middle of miles and miles of wheat fields for as far as we could see, and the fields had just been mowed. There were a few trees up ahead by the Canal Pisuerga. I told Diddo that I was going to make a break for the trees, at which point she told me she was having the same problem. Luckily we both made it to the trees just in time. I think that the milk in the coffee was spoiled. We both felt better, so we took off down the road. Thank god for the trees along the Canal Pisuerga!

There were a lot of bird hunters in the wheat fields. The sound of shotgun blast could be heard every so often.

By the time we reached the village of Boadilla del Camino, the sun was really beating down on us. As we entered the village, we noticed a small park. Next to the park was a covered patio area with several food dispensing machines and tables. We stopped, bought some cheese and olives, and, with our bread, had a great snack. In the park there was a fountain where several pilgrims had stopped for a break.

The trail went through Boadilla, then ran next to a canal for about two or so miles into Fromista. We crossed the bridge over the canal into the town of Fromista. We followed the Camino arrows to the main intersection in town. There was a tourist office there, so we stopped and got directions to the Hotel San Martin, which was just about a block away. We found the hotel with no problem. The hotel was listed as a one star. There was no one at the desk, so we went into the bar, where we found

Heather and Teresa having beers with some new friends. We joined them and an older couple from England at the table. The Brits had started the Camino in Burgos and were just doing six or so miles a day.

Heather and Teresa were headed back out onto the trail, so they took off. We did not see them after that, which was too bad. They were always in a good mood, and being around them was fun. I hope they had a *buen camino*.

We checked in and found that our room was very nice and clean. It was as nice as some three-star hotels, so I am not sure what criteria are used to rate the hotels. We took showers and washed our clothes. We were using a new method to wash our clothes. We had been using bar soap, but we were losing faith in the effectiveness of that method. We decided to use liquid hand soap or liquid shampoo. The new method was vastly superior and did a great job.

We headed down to the bar/restaurant. They did not have a Menu del Dia on Sunday, so we had a salad, steak with fries, and ice cream. Total for both of us was 24 euros. The room was a whopping 34 euros. Great room and a great meal for a great price! We headed back to the room and kicked back for a while.

Later we went out and followed the trail out of town for about a half-mile or so. We went shopping and purchased stamps, bottled water, cookies and chocolate bars. We stopped at the *albergue* and had our credentials stamped, after which we sat in the park and enjoyed the evening.

The church in Fromista, Iglesia de San Martin, is almost a thousand years old. It has undergone extensive restoration and is now a Spanish national monument and museum. It is built like a fortress and looks like it will still be standing for another thousand years.

About 7:30 p.m. we went down to the bar and had a couple of beers with the older couple. They went to the eight o'clock dinner. We stayed in the bar and ordered calamari. I tried to order two orders because we were hungry. The bartender told me to just order one plate. It was a good thing we followed his advice, because they brought us the biggest plate of calamari I have ever seen. It was very good and with the beers cost only seven euros. I could learn to like this.

We used the pay telephone in the bar to call ahead to the San Zoilo Hotel in Carrion de los Condes, our next stop. The San Zoilo is built Parador-style inside of an old monastery. Not cheap, but it looked like it might be an interesting experience.

Good day today. We covered about 16.5 miles in 7 hours. Looks like about 13 miles tomorrow with no big hills. We are going to continue with our method of early on the trail, early off the trail to avoid the afternoon heat.

Early morning view across the Meseta

Approaching Itero de la Vega

Trail along the Canal de Castilla into Fromista

Iglesia de San Martin in Fromista

CHAPTER 22

September 14, 2003-Sunday-Day 19
Fromista to Carrion de los Condes

12.5 Miles

WE got an early start to avoid the mid-day heat. We have about 13 miles to cover today. There is not a lot between Fromista and Carrion according to the guidebook, and it looks like fairly flat terrain.

It was still dark when we started. When we reached Poblacion de Campos, about 2 miles outside of Fromista, the trail became somewhat confusing, and we wound up on the alternate trail. This was not a big problem; however, at the village of Villovieco we made a detour back to the main trail that runs along the highway. The sun was just coming up when we reached the main trail.

We continued to the very small village of Villarmentero where we took a short break. Nothing was open because it was Sunday, so we just sat down at some outside tables at a closed café. Three young women from Brazil who were walking the Camino joined us. We exchanged greetings, but because of the language barrier, we didn't have much of a conversation. We were hoping we would find something open in Villalcazar, a little over 2.5 miles away.

The trail was well maintained and clearly marked, but it got boring. We reached Villalcazar and didn't find anything open. There is a beautiful church in Villalcazar, Santa Maria de la Blanca, that was built by the Knights Templar in the 13th Century. The Knights Templar used this fortified church complex as a base of operations to protect the Camino de Santiago

We stopped on a bench on the main street for a short rest. We talked to a couple from England who were walking this part of the Camino. They told us that it was cheaper for them to vacation in Spain than to travel around England.

The day had warmed up, and I was feeling tired, I think because we had not eaten anything, and walking along a road through mile after mile of wheat fields doesn't stimulate you much.

We arrived in Carrion about 11:45 a.m. We normally head right for the hotel, but we were both so hungry we stopped at the first bar in town and had coffee and *tortilla*s. A poster on the wall of the bar advertised a three-day fiesta that was taking place in Carrion. There was a lot of activity on the street making preparations for the events that were going to take place today. We decided to head for our hotel.

The San Zoilo is located on the far side of Carrion, so we got the tour of the town. At the edge of Carrion, we went over a beautiful bridge that crosses the Rio Carrion. A short distance later, we located the Monastery San Zoilo. This magnificent building is a 16th Century renaissance cloister that has been designated as a national monument. The hotel has been built into the original structure, much like the government-run Paradors of Spain. After locating the impressive lobby, we checked in and headed for our room, 65 euros. The room was great, and just walking through the building was very interesting.

I was more tired than usual. I don't know why, maybe just the boredom of today's hike. We washed our clothes, took showers, and I soaked my feet. We headed down to the hotel restaurant for a late lunch.

The restaurant was a very upscale place. When we walked in, there were only a few customers. We asked for a table for two. The hostess asked if we had reservations. I couldn't believe it. The place was huge and was just about empty. We advised her that we did not have reservations. She left us and looked around the restaurant. She came back and took us to a nice table. I kept thinking that all of this was for show. Within a few minutes after we were seated, however, the place filled up. It looked like mostly local people. This must be the place to go after church. We had a great meal: salad with baked goat cheese, lamb chops, and ice cream. The meal cost 55 euros for both of us.

We walked around the grounds of the monastery, then took the trail out of town for a short distance. It appeared to be well marked, with no surprises. We were both tired, so we headed back to the room to square away our gear and rest up. We watched our usual Spanish soap opera and the weather report in Spanish. They also had CNN Europe, which is in English, so we caught up on the world news.

It seems that every so often, we have a low-energy day. When you get to where you are going, you just want to kick back, write in your journal, square away your gear, read, send postcards, etc. This seemed to be one of those days. We did close to 13 miles today in a little over 5 hours.

We have a long day tomorrow to Terradillos de Templarios. According to the map, there are some up and downs, but it's mostly flat, with not much to see along the way. There are no hotels or hostels in Terradillos de Templarios or anywhere in the area, so we are planning to stay in the *albergue*. We planned on taking off early, so we had to inform the desk clerk because they lock the doors at the hotel. They said that they would have the security guard meet us in the morning to let us out.

Camino into Villalcazar

Santa Maria de la Blanca in Villalcazar

Bridge over the Rio Carrion in Carrion de los Condes

Monastery San Zoilo

CHAPTER 23

September 15, 2003-Monday-Day 20
Carrion de los Condes to Terradillos de Templarios

17 Miles

THE security guard was waiting for us in the lobby to let us out. It was cool enough for our jackets. We had to use our headlamps because less than a block from the hotel we were in the countryside, and it was very dark. This is the best part of the day for me, especially here on the Meseta. I am full of energy, it is cool, and we always make good time.

There were not a lot of pilgrims on the trail at this time of the morning. I don't know why, but most people seem to wait for daylight before they take off, which means that they are on the trail during the hottest part of the day. It also means that they miss the sun coming up which out here, on the Meseta is a beautiful sight.

One couple passed us just outside of town. The trail was somewhat the same as yesterday: straight, flat, and boring. I tried Diddo's breathing exercise-concentrating on my breathing, counting as I inhaled and exhaled. Then I concentrated on relaxing my body. After a while, the miles just passed by. It worked well and gave me something to do on the long stretches.

We stopped at nine o'clock at the side of the trail for a snack of bread, cheese, Ruffles, and a candy bar. After we took off, it was back to the breathing exercise.

Each section of the Camino has its own challenge. Out here on the Meseta, it tends to be boredom. In the mountains, it's steep up and downs. In the cities, it's noise, traffic, and people. I think that this is one of the unique things about the Camino. About the time you are tired of the landscape it changes, and you have new challenges.

We came over a rise, and could see the village of Calzadilla de la Cueza. We couldn't believe that we had come this far. I guess the breathing exercises work! Calzadilla de la Cueza is one of the only villages on today's trek, and we were really hoping for a bar or café so we could take a break and get something to eat.

Diddo seemed a little beat today. Her hip was bothering her for some reason, and she had a bump on her forehead that she thought was from an insect bite. When we slept on the *albergue*'s kitchen floor a couple of days ago in Hornillos, she felt something bite her, then saw a spider moving away. It was a pretty good-sized bump.

As we walked into Calzadilla de la Cueza, there was a sign pointing the way to a bar around the corner. We followed the arrows to the place that also had a hostel that looked pretty nice. We went in and had coffee, several slices of *tortilla*, and some bread that had melted cheese, ham, and green beans on it. It was all really good. This was a very refreshing break, but it was getting hot outside so we hit the trail.

After leaving Calzadilla de la Cueza, the trail splits, with an alternate route going by the ruins of Santa Maria de las Tiendas. We decided to stay on the main trail that went along the highway. There was a steep hill, followed by a short downhill into the village of Ledigos. We continued on because Terradillos de Templarios was only about two miles ahead, and we wanted to reach the *albergue* before it filled up.

After Ledigos, the trail started uphill, next to the main highway. These two miles seemed to take forever. There was not a lot to see. The sun was right overhead. It was hot, and there was no shade. After the long, never-ending uphill, we reached a plateau. Shortly thereafter, we reached Terradillos de Templarios. It is a small village, with not a lot going on. We headed down the main street and found the *albergue*.

We checked in and got two of the last beds before they started using the overflow area. The cost was seven euros each. The woman who ran the place seemed like a no-nonsense kind of person. She took us to our beds, which were in a room with three other beds. The room looked nice and fairly clean.

There were three Germans, two males and one female, bunking in the room. We had seen them on the trail before. They were about our age. One of the guys looked like he was having real problems with his feet. He stayed in bed most of the time, and when he did walk around, it looked really painful.

We took showers and then washed our clothes in an outside clothes-washing area that used an electric pump to pump well water. They also had pay washing machines, but we used our liquid shampoo hand-washing method-why change now? We hung our clothes on a clothesline, then just kicked back in the patio area with everyone else. There was not much else to do in Terradillos de Templarios.

We went to the dining area and had a couple of beers. They opened a small store that they had in the *albergue*, so we bought some bottled water. The *albergue* store is the only store in town.

The three Brazilian gals showed up with Lester, the dentist from Canada. We heard on the trail that they had caused a disturbance at the *albergue* in Carrion. They came in late from a round of drinking and raised hell. The first thing they did when they arrived in Terradillos de Templarios was to get into an argument with the manager of the *albergue* because they wanted to get their beds for free. From what we could make out, they were claiming poverty and felt that the *albergue* should provide them with free space. The *albergue* manager wasn't buying any of this. This *albergue*, like some on the Camino, was a commercial establishment. Lester stepped in and said that he would pay for their beds. He pulled out some euros and paid the bill. Maybe it's just the old cop in me, but looking at the clothes these gals were wearing, stylish and expensive, and the gear they were carrying, I think that they were taking advantage of people.

The two American gals that had been walking with Lester when we met outside of Hornillos also showed up and checked in.

During the early evening, we took a long walk out of town following the trail. It was a little confusing, so we wanted to really scout it out. We followed the trail for about a mile, which turned out to be a good idea. It would have been a mess to try to figure it out in the dark.

Back at the *albergue*, we had dinner in the dining room at eight o'clock. During dinner, we talked to a young Brazilian man who was seated at the table. He told everyone that he was a professional racecar driver. He said that the stress and strain of high-speed racing was wearing on him, so he was doing the Camino to get his mind right. He claimed to be doing very high mileage every day.

It looked like we might get a good night's sleep. We have a long day tomorrow, about 20 miles to El Burgo Ranero. We are planning an early start to beat the heat. Before going to bed, we got our gear together so that we could get ready in the hallway area in the morning. This way we would not disturb the others in the room. At about ten o'clock, it was lights out, and we hit the sack.

CHAPTER 24

September 16, 2003-Tuesday-Day 21
Terradillos de Templarios to El Burgo Ranero

20 Miles

WE got about two minutes of sleep last night. The German guy with the feet problems was sleeping at the foot of my bed. When the lights went out, he started to snore. This guy was the loudest snorer I have ever heard. After about five minutes, the German woman, who I think was his wife, grabbed her walking stick, beat it against the floor, and yelled at the top of her lungs for him to stop snoring. He would stop for about a minute, start snoring again, then the whole process would start all over. After about an hour of this, the wife stopped her part of the disturbance. I guess she just gave up. The snorer continued to snore. The snore turned into a snoring/choking that became louder and more disgusting. After choking for a while, he would get up and go to the restroom, where he could be heard vomiting, farting, and making every other bodily noise that you can think of. This went on all night. Diddo had to go to the restroom once during the night, and, of the three restrooms, she picked the one that this guy used. It was covered with vomit.

We got up at 5:30 a.m. and moved our gear to the hallway to get ready. We were on the trail a short time later. It was a good thing that we checked the trail the day before, because the way out of town was confusing. There was one other couple in front of us who got lost right away. We put them on the right trail. Nice, cool hiking weather, but you could feel that it was going to be a hot one today.

We made good time to Sahagun, arriving a little after sunup. We found a coffee shop and stopped for coffee and *magdalanas*. We both were tired because of so little sleep. We found our way through Sahagun, which is a pretty good-sized town. The trail was poorly marked through Sahagun, so we had to keep our eyes peeled.

A bridge at the edge of town took us over the Rio Cea. The sun was up by this time, and the heat was on. Outside of town, we saw the Brazilian racecar driver from last night. He was asleep on a bench. I didn't think that he was going to make all of the miles he was talking about last night.

After about two and a quarter miles, we came to a fork in the trail. One route takes you to Calzadilla de los Hermanillos, the other to El Burgo Ranero. We were headed to El Burgo Ranero. There is a rest area by the trail marker, so we took a break and had some bread and cheese, with a candy bar for dessert. The trail sign was confusing, but we made our best guess and took off.

The trail to El Burgo Ranero had some up and downs, but was mostly flat. There was almost no shade or relief of any kind from the heat. The other problem out here on the Meseta is that most of the time you can see the trail for miles ahead. After a while, this starts to drive you a little crazy. You can see where you are going, but it may be hours away.

We reached the outskirts of Bercianos, where we found some shade trees and a bench. We stopped for a short break. An old man, with a cane of course, walked up to us, and in the usual English, Spanish, and sign language, we had a conversation. He informed us that his son is a professor who speaks Spanish, English and Russian. He was very interested in our trip, where we were from, and what we thought of Spain. While we were talking, a group of tourists, from Belgium came by. They looked too refreshed to be pilgrims. It turned out that they were part of a bus tour.

We said goodbye to the old fellow and took off. At a bar in Bercianos, we passed several of our fellow pilgrims who were taking a break to get out of the sun. We wanted to get to El Burgo Ranero and get to our room, take a shower, and get off of the trail, so we kept going. This turned into an endless march under the hot, glaring sun. We stopped once more, no shade, by a stream, then took off.

After a long uphill, we saw El Burgo Ranero in the distance by a freeway ramp. There also appeared to be a small airport. We kept going, but our destination did not seem to get any closer. I ran out of water about the time we walked under the freeway.

El Burgo Ranero was only about a half mile away, but it seemed to take forever to reach the main street. We started to follow confusing directions to the hostel but finally gave up and asked directions. After about ten minutes, we found our hostel. It was located just across the street from the *albergue.*

We went into the bar, which was very busy. It appeared to be mostly locals. We saw a doorway with a sign that said "Hostal." We started through the door, but were stopped by the bartender and a customer who asked us where we were going. They seemed a little irritated. I explained, the best I could, that we had a reservation. They relaxed and called a woman who was at the other end of the bar. She came over, got our names, confirmed the reservation, and took us to our room. As always, she was very nice. The room was on the third floor and was one of only a few rooms that had a bathroom and shower.

As seemed to be the custom, she left and told us to stop by and pay for the room later. The room was clean, but we had to laugh at the design. The ceiling slanted from the door area to the window. You could not stand straight up in most of the room. The bathroom was so small that you could barely turn around. Nevertheless, it was out of the sun, fairly clean, had a shower and toilet, and no snoring, choking, retching, farting roommates.

We were both beat. More beat than any day before. I know that I felt dehydrated. We took a couple of large Ibuprofen. We have enough experience with hiking to know that a day like today can kick your butt for days to come with sore muscles and aches and pains.

I was the entertainment because every time I turned around, I would hit my head on the ceiling, causing both of us to break out in laughter.

We didn't want to miss lunch, so before we showered we headed downstairs to the hostel restaurant: salad, beefsteak, and french fries. The beefsteak was so tough that we could hardly eat it. So much for fine dining in El Burgo Ranero.

We headed upstairs, took showers, and washed our clothes. We crashed for about an hour, after which we went out to walk around the village. We stopped at the *albergue* and had our credentials stamped, then went to the store. We bought bottled water, cookies, and shampoo (to wash clothes). It was still very warm, so we also got some ice cream cones. It was nice sitting outside the store, watching the world go by, and eating ice cream.

We took the trail out of town, and found it to be well marked and easy to follow. Back at the *albergue*, we checked for Lester or any of the Brazilian gals but didn't see them. I think they may have stopped in Bercianos, where we last saw them in the bar.

The *albergue* was completely full. We went over to the hostel bar, sat outside, and had a couple of beers, along with a ham and cheese *bocadillo* and olives.

It was a long night last night, and a long day today. It took us about 7.5 hours to cover almost 20 miles. I think today was one of the hardest days so far. We have a shorter day tomorrow, about 12 miles or so to Mansilla de las Mulas. We made reservations at a three-star hotel in Mansilla de las Mulas. We are both looking forward to a shorter day and a nice hotel.

We relaxed the rest of the evening, then hit the rack early. We wanted to get an early start in the morning to avoid a replay of today.

Ermita Virgen del Puente-just outside of Sahagun

CHAPTER 25

September 17, 2003-Wednesday-Day 22
El Burgo Ranero to Mansilla de las Mulas

12.5 Miles

WE both had a good night's sleep. I didn't hit my head any more on the low ceiling; I guess I must have adjusted to the room. We were up early and on the trail by 6:30 a.m. We made great time in the dark. The weather was cool and perfect for hiking, flat walking, with a few slight up and downs. We made the railroad crossing, one of the only landmarks on this section, in two hours, a distance of about six miles.

The sun came up at 8:05 a.m. It is so flat that we could see forever in every direction.

A short time after sunup, we found a rest area with cement tables. We stopped for a short break and a snack: bread, cheese, candy and cookies.

A short time later, we came over a crest and could see Mansilla de las Mulas in the distance. This was going to be one of those days where we could see where we were headed for hours!

There was a short downhill into the village of Reliegos. As we were entering the village, we noticed that there were homes built underground. The roofs are made of sod and are just above ground level. The doors are below ground level.

We took a short break in Reliegos at a small bar in the center of the village. I had coffee solo (without milk). I like the coffee this way better, and I don't have to worry about spoiled milk.

When we took off, we could see Mansilla de las Mulas about four miles away across a flat valley. After what seemed like forever, we went over the freeway on an overpass into the streets of Mansilla de las Mulas.

We walked to a main intersection and tried to figure out where our hotel was located. We stopped a couple of people to ask for directions. One man said that there was no such hotel. The next guy knew the hotel we were looking for and gave us directions. It turned out that the hotel was about a half mile out of town, so we had a little farther to go.

We followed the directions to the hotel, crossed the busy freeway, and finally located the place. We found out after reaching the hotel that we had taken the long route. There was a shortcut, via a tunnel under the freeway.

We arrived at about 11:00 a.m. The hotel was a nice place, and our room was great. The cost was 54 euros. There seemed to be several Guardia Civil Officers hanging around the hotel, so at least, I guess, we were safe.

Before we did anything else, we decided to take a walk into town. We needed to get some supplies, and I wanted to get a brush to clean our boots. They were covered with the white, chalk-like dirt that is common on the Meseta.

We took the shortcut into town, and while we were there, walked the route out of town for the next morning. We found a store and bought bread, candy bars, canned red bell peppers, and bottled water. I found a paintbrush I could use to clean our boots. We located the *albergue* and figured we might as well get our credentials stamped while we were there. There was a group of very tired-looking pilgrims waiting outside. Turned out that they didn't open until 2:30, and they were making the pilgrims wait outside. We decided to get our credentials stamped at the hotel.

As we walked around, we noticed that the streets of Mansilla de las Mulas were covered with trash, and there seemed to be about a million gnats in the air. Someone told us that they had just had a fiesta, and that was the reason for all of the trash.

It was getting hot, and we were both beat. I think that we were both still feeling the effects of yesterday's trek. I needed a shower and some food. We headed back to the hotel and got cleaned up.

At the hotel bar/restaurant, we had the Menu del Dia that consisted of salad, beefsteak with fries, and ice cream. We also had a couple of ice-cold beers and bottled water. The bill came to nine euros each. The food was very good, one of the best steaks so far.

While I was eating, my fingers did that muscle seizure thing again. I think this was from using the walking stick, but I don't know for sure.

Back up at the room, we made a deal that Diddo would wash the clothes, and I would take the boots outside and clean them. There was a small park with a fountain next to the hotel. I headed over there to scrub the boots clean.

We talked yesterday about doing a complete cleaning of all of our gear and packs. This seemed like a good place to do it. We unloaded everything from our packs, cleaned them, and then cleaned all of our gear. We then re-packed everything. This action was prompted by numerous, very small red marks we have been finding on our bodies. They looked like some type of flea bites. We may have picked something up in one of the *albergue*s. We also unpacked and aired out our sleeping bags.

Today we covered about 12.5 miles in 5 hours. We were a little tired, but we felt like we had recovered from yesterday.

Tomorrow we head into Leon, one of the largest cities on the Camino. It is about 12 miles. We have reservations at a four-star A.C. Hotel. We tried for a room at the Leon Parador, but they were full.

Looking east back toward El Burgo Ranero

Looking west toward Mansilla de las Mulas

CHAPTER 26

September 18, 2003-Thursday-Day 23
Mansilla de las Mulas to Leon

12 Miles

WE took off early through Mansilla de las Mulas, and over a bridge out of town that crosses the Rio Esla. The trail went alongside or on the shoulder, of a very busy highway. There was not much to see. We really had to keep an eye on the traffic. On some of the bridges it got a little scary. There was hardly any shoulder to walk on, and there were lots of big trucks whizzing by. We crossed the bridges as fast as possible.

We both seemed to be in a low-energy mood today. The long haul two days ago was still kicking our butts. We wanted to get to Leon as early as possible, although we were not looking forward to being in a big city.

The trail was flat for the most part, but boring. We went through Villarente where the trail markers seemed to disappear for a while, but we continued on. I knew that the road would wind up in Leon one way or another. Outside of Villarente, we found the trail markers again. The trail went off of the road for almost three miles, so we got a little break from the traffic. We stopped in an industrial area outside of Leon and had a snack while sitting on old broken chunks of cement.

There was a long uphill just prior to Valdelafuente. All of the pilgrims seemed to be on the same part of the trail, so we all struggled up the hill in the hot sun together. The trail then crossed the main highway, which seemed to be as busy as a freeway, with lots of high-speed traffic. Getting across the highway was a real adventure. The trail went alongside of the highway on the shoulder for a short distance, then over another freeway on a footbridge. After crossing the footbridge, we were in Leon proper.

We stopped for a minute outside what looked like a hospital to check our map and take a short break. As we were standing there, a guy walked up to us from the hospital lawn area and started yelling at us to leave. We figured out about that time that the place was a mental facility, so we took off rather quickly.

When we reached the busy downtown area of Leon, things got a little confusing. The Camino was well marked; however, the hotel we were looking for was about four blocks off of the Camino. We asked one man if he knew where the A.C. Hotel was located. He seemed confused, and would only give us directions for the Camino. We followed our map and after a few short detours we found the hotel. It turned out to be a very impressive place.

We got checked in-125 euros a night, but well worth it. All of the A.C. Hotels have a room stocked with drinks, sandwiches and snacks that is open to the guests. Everything is free. We took showers, washed our clothes, and then just sat around and basked in the luxury of the place.

I still didn't feel one hundred percent. I just seemed to be dragging, but couldn't put my finger on why.

We headed out to find the *albergue* and get our credentials stamped. We also wanted to check the trail out of the city for tomorrow morning. We left the hotel and went back to where we had turned off the Camino. We followed the yellow arrows through the city to the *albergue*.

When we presented our credentials to the *albergue* manager, he commented in Spanish that we seemed to stay in a lot of hotels. He continued with his comments in an attempt to bust our chops about staying in hotels instead of staying in the *albergues*. At first, I didn't pick up on his attitude, so I explained to him that all of the *albergues* we had encountered had been overcrowded and filled past capacity. He said that he knew this, but that the *albergues* would always make room for more. We didn't want to get into an argument with the guy, so we just waited until he stamped our credentials, and then took off.

In my humble opinion, this guy's attitude really sucked. From day one, we felt that we could afford to pay for a hostel or hotel. We didn't come to Spain looking for an inexpensive vacation with the idea of taking advantage of the *albergues* as a form of free or cheap lodging. The way I looked at it was that if we took a space in an *albergue*, that meant that someone who couldn't afford a hotel room was sleeping on the floor, or in some cases, outside. I would think that the *albergue* staff members would appreciate people who didn't impact their system unnecessarily. (As a matter of fact, we would encounter *albergue* managers later who thanked us for staying in hotels, thus freeing up beds in the *albergue*.)

Along the Camino, we encountered people who felt very strongly that to be a pilgrim, you had to suffer. The level of suffering you must endure depended on who you were talking to. To some folks, walking twelve to twenty miles a day over a long period of time is just not enough suffering. They felt that at the end of the day, you should not enjoy any type of comfort.

When we left the *albergue*, we headed for the cathedral. En route, we found a restaurant, kind of a tourist place, and decided to stop and eat lunch. I had pizza, and Diddo had the lamb. The meal was just OK and cost 27 euros, with beers.

After lunch, we followed the yellow arrows to the cathedral. We stopped there to take pictures and look around. We continued on, got lost for a block, but then got back on track. We did find a bookstore with English language books, but they were closed for the siesta, just my luck. We continued to follow the trail, which turned into a very long walk.

We reached the Leon Parador, which appeared to be a very impressive place. The map showed a shortcut from our hotel to this location, so we backtracked that way, thinking that we would use this route in the morning.

During the latter part of this walk, I started to feel poorly. My stomach went from bad to worse, and that was just the start. By the time we got back to the room, I could barely move. The pizza I had for lunch felt like it had expanded one hundred times in my stomach. As the evening went on, I had several bouts of diarrhea. This did not bring any relief. At about ten o'clock, I just made it to the bathroom before I started to vomit. This went on until there was nothing left in my system. I felt better afterwards, but very weak. I was really worried, not only about tomorrow, but about the rest of the trip. I had not been this sick to my stomach in many years, and I couldn't help but wonder if there was something really wrong with me.

We decided to see how I felt in the morning before we made any big decision

Just outside of Leon

Leon Cathedral

Leon Cathedral

Resting pilgrim monument in front of Leon Parador

CHAPTER 27

September 19, 2003-Friday-Day 24
Leon to Nowhere

I didn't sleep any during the night. My stomach felt better, but I still didn't feel very good. I drank as much water as possible because I knew I was dehydrated.

When morning came, I knew I wasn't going anywhere. Diddo went down to the desk and got the room for one more night. We went out for a short walk and bought some bananas and peaches. I was looking for something like a Gatorade-type drink, with no luck.

When we got back to the room, I hit the sack. Diddo went out to see some of the sights and look for some Gatorade or something like it. I slept all day. When I woke up, I felt much better. Diddo did find a sports-type drink. I drank that and all of the water I could take. I ate the bananas, but not much else. By that night, I felt better.

Our plan was to hit the trail and see how far I could go. We made a hotel reservation at Villadangos del Paramo. There are two routes out of Leon. One route leads to Mazarife where there is a small *albergue*, but, according to the guidebook, not much else.

The other route leads to Villadangos del Paramo, which is just short of 12 miles away. Our plan was to take the Villadangos del Paramo route. I was really hoping that I felt OK in the morning, because we both wanted to get back on the trail.

CHAPTER 28

September 20, 2003-Saturday-Day 25
Leon to Villadangos del Paramo

13 Miles

SLEPT great all night, and in the morning I felt much better. I guess it was just some bad food. I just ate bread and bananas because I didn't want to push my luck.

We were up early and took off at 6:20 a.m. We took the short route that went along a river park in the city as far as the Parador. We picked up the main Camino there and crossed the bridge over the Rio Bernesga. The trail markings were not that good, so we really had to pay attention and keep our eye on the map. It seemed like we were walking through the city for a long time.

We made good time to La Virgen del Camino. I felt good, and it was a nice day. We stopped at a small café/bar in La Virgen del Camino. Diddo had coffee and a roll. I didn't want to chance it, so I passed. We saw Bill walk by. We had not seen him for several days, since before Burgos.

The trail out of La Virgen del Camino had changed since our guidebook was published; however, there were many other pilgrims and the new trail was pretty well marked. This is where the trail splits between the Mazarife route and the route to Villadangos del Paramo. The new trail went around and under a freeway interchange. Once we got through that section, the trail was very straightforward with a fairly level grade, mostly next to the road.

We went through the villages of Valverde and San Miguel. In San Miguel, we walked by a store where an older man had set out fruit for pilgrims. We didn't take any, but Diddo thanked him for his kindness.

It was great hiking weather, with just enough cloud cover to keep the temperature down and the sun off of us. Between San Miguel and Villadangos del Paramo we stopped for a short break. I ate a banana, then continued the short distance to Villadangos del Paramo.

We arrived at our hotel at 11:30 a.m. It turned out that the hotel was way on the east side of town. The door to the hotel was locked, so we rang the buzzer. A male voice came on the intercom. We informed him that we had a reservation. He buzzed us in. Over the intercom, the male voice told us to take a key. All of the hotel keys were on the desk. This was a little confusing, kind of a check-in by remote control. The clerk finally came to the counter. He was in the process of buckling his pants. I guess he must have been in the restroom. He gave us our key, so we headed to the room. There did not seem to be anyone else in the place. The room was fine.

We kicked back for a while, then washed our clothes and took showers. We headed out to find the *albergue* to get our credentials stamped. It turned out that it was about a mile down the road, where the main part of town was located. We found the *albergue* and had our credentials stamped. The *albergue* manager, a female, thanked us for staying in a hotel. What a difference from the guy in Leon!

We walked the trail out of town. It seemed to be well marked and easy to follow. Even though it was siesta time, we found a small store open, so we picked up some supplies we needed: bread, cheese, salami, pastries and chocolate donuts.

While we were walking around, a man standing on the main corner in town gave us a card advertising a restaurant. We headed over to the place, which was about a block off the road. Looked kind of weird to me. The front of the place was normal, but the rear part of the restaurant was built underground. We went inside and took a seat. We had the Menu del Dia; salad, which seemed to be all tomatoes, fish and french fries, with an apple for dessert. The fish was good and seemed to sit well with me.

We took the long walk back to the hotel and found that we were still the only customers. We wanted to pay our bill so we could leave early in the morning. I went downstairs, but there was still no desk clerk. I tried the intercom, which was answered by a man. I tried to explain that I wanted to pay our bill, but because of the language barrier, I didn't have any luck. A cleaning woman showed up, and I tried to explain again, with the same results. I went to the room and got Diddo, who was able to get the point across. I paid the cleaning woman, 44 euros.

Later I went over to the hostel that was located next to the hotel. It looked like it was part of the same complex. It turned out that all of the staff was at the hostel. I used the pay phone at the hostel to make a reservation at a hotel in Astorga, our next planned stop.

Later we went to the hostel bar and had a couple of beers. After heading back to the room, we watched our Spanish soap opera and the weather report. It looked like there may be some rain ahead.

CHAPTER 29

September 21, 2003-Sunday-Day 26
Villadangos to Astorga

17 Miles

WE both slept well and were up early. We were on the road by 6:15 a.m. We had a long day ahead of us, a little over 17 miles.

When we left the hotel, we noticed that the place was full. The parking lot was filled with cars, most of them very nice cars. I never did figure out what the deal was.

The trail was very straightforward through Villadangos. It went through a campground area then next to the road, where it continued into San Martin. It seemed like it took forever to reach San Martin. When I checked, however, it looked like we were making good time. We stopped at a little park across the street from the *albergue* and ate some cookies.

We continued on, the trail staying next to the road. Good trail, but somewhat boring. On the trail we encountered an older man who did not look very good. He was leaning against one of the trail markers and appeared to be having trouble breathing. We stopped, and Diddo asked him if he was OK. He answered in English that he was fine. We were concerned, but it looked like he had things under control, so we continued on.

We reached Hospital del Orbigo a little after sun up. The bridge leading into town was beautiful and is one of the oldest medieval bridges in Spain. The bridge is famous for jousting matches that took place there in the 15th Century. A famous knight, Don Suero de Quinones, challenged any and all knights who crossed the bridge. Knights from all over Europe took up the challenge, but none were successful against Don Suero de Quinones.

After crossing the bridge, we looked for a bar or café to get something to eat. Since it was Sunday, we knew that there would not be much open. An old man directed us down a side street to the only open bar. We went in and, to our surprise they had toast with jelly. We had coffee and two orders of toast.

As we walked through town, we noticed that everything looked very clean and nice. We ran into Bill in the center of town. He was with the older gentleman we had seen earlier. He still did not look very good. Bill told us later that this fellow had Parkinson's disease but wanted to walk the Camino. Talk about courage. There is a good lesson in this for everyone. We are in good health, but sometimes we worry about the rain, our feet, the condition of the trail, and what is up ahead. Here was this gentleman with Parkinson's disease and he was out here walking in the same conditions. There are always lessons to be learned!

There are two routes out of Hospital del Orbigo; we took what is known as the road route. After leaving town we went through cornfields, then back to the main highway. The trail was as straight as a string, but in very good condition. We passed people who were working in vineyards. It looked like a family enterprise.

I was starting to run out of gas. I think that I was still a little weak from two days ago. We stopped at a bus stop bench and took a short break. We met Jean Pierre, a French Canadian who was also sitting there. He seemed a little dejected. He told us that he had been making very good time on the Camino, but that he was now suffering from shin splints so severe that he could not walk without a great deal of pain. He said that he was going to wait for a bus to take him into Astorga. I could tell that he was not happy with this decision. I guess everyone feels the same way about the possibility of not being able to finish the Camino. A few minutes later, Bill showed up and sat down with us to take a break.

After we were rested, we said goodbye and good luck to Jean Pierre, and hit the trail. There were two very long uphill climbs, but, as usual, talking to Bill as we walked made the miles go by without much effort.

We reached the high point of the day, and Bill decided to take a break and eat something. We went on, to a cross high on a hill, where we got our first view of Astorga. There were some benches there, so we took a break and had a snack.

Astorga looked close, so we took off, hoping to get there early. Looks are deceiving. We went downhill into San Justo, a little town just outside of Astorga. We crossed a bridge, after which the trail went away from the main road. The road looked like a better route, but we followed the yellow arrows. The trail went through fields, and mud, then behind some warehouses. It connected back to the road just below the Astorga city walls. Just when we were really tired, the road went up what must be the steepest hill on the Camino. It was only about two blocks long, but straight up, and a real killer. Huffing and puffing, we finally entered the town of Astorga.

We followed our map to the central plaza where our hotel was located. It was a beautiful place and a welcome end to a long day. We got checked in (65 euros), then headed to our room. Everything was great. We were a little beat, but felt good about the long mileage, seventeen plus miles in seven and a half hours.

We did our usual duties, showers and clothes washing, then headed to the hotel restaurant. The meal was good, except we tried cold watermelon soup. I didn't like it, but Diddo thought it was great. I had veal cutlets with melted blue cheese that was excellent. Forty-five euros for both of us including wine and water.

We went to the room and crashed for a while, then headed out to the *albergue* to get our credentials stamped. We checked the route out of town, which seemed to be well marked and easy to follow. We strolled around town taking in the sights. Astorga seemed to be a busy place. We used the pay phone to make a reservation at the hostel in Rabanal, our next stop.

One of the only times someone became upset with us occurred here. We sat at an outside table in the plaza to have a drink before we headed to the room for the night. The plaza was very busy with locals and tourists. The waitress came over, I ordered a beer and Diddo ordered a Vino Tinto, or red wine. The waitress seemed upset before she came to our table. In Spanish, she asked what brand of red wine Diddo wanted. Diddo told her it didn't matter. This seemed to really upset the gal. We noticed that as other people ordered, they seem to get the same treatment. She must have been having a bad day.

Tomorrow is a shorter day, about thirteen miles; however, we are starting up into the mountains so it may not be that easy. We are hoping the good weather holds.

Feeling better the second day out of Leon

Bridge into Hospital de Orbigo

Diddo crossing the bridge

Under ground buildings

Under ground buildings

Crucero Santo Toribio outside of Astorga

Downhill into San Justo

Astorga in distance

CHAPTER 30

September 22, 2003-Monday-Day 27
Astorga to Rabanal

14 Miles

IT rained for a short time in the middle of the night. We were up early. We ate some bread before taking off, a practice we started in Leon. It seemed to help keep up the energy level early in the morning.

We were on the trail at 6:30 a.m. The trail markers were OK on the route out of Astorga, but we had to keep our eyes peeled after leaving town. Steady, long, uphill grade into the foothills where Rabanal is located. The weather was cool, cloudy, and it looked like rain.

When we reached Santa Catalina, we looked for an open bar to get some coffee, but everything was still closed. One of the problems with our early starts was that most cafes and bars did not open until at least nine o'clock.

We made it into El Ganso about an hour later. There were two places open for business, both of which were filled with pilgrims. We opted for one that was in a house. Two women had sat up a small café inside of their home and were serving coffee and *bocadillos*. We had coffee and a *bocadillo con huevos* (egg sandwich). One sandwich was more than two people could eat. A German guy sitting next to us ordered a brandy! He really seemed to enjoy it. I don't know how he could drink brandy that early in the morning.

It had warmed up enough to take off our jackets, but about five minutes out of El Ganso the wind kicked up again, so we stopped to put them back on. There were a couple of picnic benches outside of town, so we stopped there to change. This sounds simple, putting on or taking off a jacket, but it involves taking off your pack, putting on the jacket, putting the pack back on, and making the adjustments. While we were doing this, a couple of the biggest dogs I had ever seen came into the picnic table area. They had been tending a flock of sheep on the other side of the road. A woman pilgrim sitting at one of the other tables became frightened of the dogs and asked us if they were dangerous. Like I would know! We told her we had no idea, but we got out of there as fast as possible. I didn't want to mess with big Spanish dogs!

The weather continued to look bad, but it had not rained on us so far. The trail was a steady but not steep, uphill into Rabanal. Nice trail, mostly next to the road. During the last two or so miles into Rabanal, the grade got steeper and steeper. A real butt kicker. We were glad to see the village up ahead. The Camino went up the main street of Rabanal to the hostel where we had reservations. It was very steep, but at least the end was in sight.

We reached Rabanal around noon, fourteen miles in five and a half hours. We found the El Refugio Hostal, which was located across the street from the church and *albergue*. Forty-five euros for a nice, clean, warm room. The El Refugio Hostal is a family-run place.

We took showers, but instead of washing all of our clothes, we only washed our socks. We thought that we might need the extra shirt tomorrow because of the cold weather.

We went to lunch at about 2:30 p.m. The restaurant/bar at the hostel was a very busy place. The Menu del Dia was great: very hearty vegetable soup, calamari with fries, and ice cream. The meal was eight and a half euros each, including wine.

We walked across the street to the *albergue* to get our credentials stamped. By now it was very cold, windy, and cloudy. It turned out that there are two *albergue*s in town because this is such a major stopping point before crossing the mountains. The Confraternity of St. James runs the main *albergue*. An older couple from England and an older man from Texas were running the place. We stopped and talked to them for a while. They volunteer for two weeks at a time. They said that it was hard work, but they found it enjoyable and rewarding. After the pilgrims leave in the morning, they spend most of the day cleaning the place up, washing bedding, etc. At 3:00 p.m., they start checking in new pilgrims.

We walked back downhill to a store we passed on the way into town. Turned out to be a very nice little store where we picked up bottled water, bananas, and bread.

We headed to the room for a nap and watched Spanish TV. No CNN today. The weather report didn't look very good for tomorrow.

Later in the evening, we went back out and checked the trail out of town. There was some construction going on just as the trail left the village. It could be confusing in the dark.

We went over to the other *albergue* just to take a look, and it seemed like a nice place.

Rabanal is an interesting village, rich in history. Most of the buildings are made of rock and look very substantial. The whole town has an outpost feeling to it. Rabanal was, in fact, a Templar stronghold protecting the pass through the mountains we would be crossing tomorrow. Even though Rabanal is located only a few miles from Astorga, you get the feeling that you are in the middle of nowhere.

Before heading back to the room, we stopped for a couple of beers at the hostel bar. I really enjoyed this place. There was a big fire going in the fireplace, and it had a very comfortable feel to it. The bar also seemed to be the meeting place for everyone in town, both locals and pilgrims.

The highest point of the whole Camino is on tomorrow's route, and it is an area noted for bad weather. We were planning to wear several layers of clothing. We were hoping for good weather, but it looked like rain.

Approaching Rabanal

El Rufigo Hostal in Rabanal

Main street Rabanal

Church in Rabanal

CHAPTER 31

September 23, 2003-Tuesday-Day 28
Rabanal to Molinaseca

17 Miles

IT rained most of the night and was so windy that it woke us up several times. Even with that, we slept well.

Before heading out, we put on three layers of clothing, plus a jacket and long pants. We took off at about 6:30 a.m. It looked like we were the only ones on the trail this early. When we got outside, we could see the stars. It didn't look like there was a cloud in the sky, but it was too dark to tell for sure. The wind had died down. It was cold, but not as bad as we thought it was going to be.

We went through the construction area and headed out of town. After about a mile or so we became concerned. We were the only ones on the trail, and we had not seen any markers for quite a while. It was so dark that it was hard to get our bearings. We couldn't see our hands in front of our faces. Our whole world was what we could see in the beam of our headlamps. It was somewhat disorienting because we were unable to pick out any landmarks to fix our position.

We stopped and checked the map, which indicated that we should cross a paved road soon. We held our breath until we came to the paved road. Shortly thereafter, we found the trail markers. What a relief!

It was a steady uphill, but not nearly as bad as we had expected. The way people talked about this section of the Camino had us thinking that we were in for a very steep, difficult climb.

We wanted to reach Cruz de Ferro at sunup, but it didn't look like we were going to make it in time. The morning was nice, and warmer than we expected. We started to overheat and sweat with all the layers of clothing we had on.

About sunup we reached the village of Foncebadon, which appeared to be mostly abandoned. We were disappointed that we didn't make it to Cruz de Ferro in time to see the sun come up.

Cruz de Ferro, as I said earlier, is the highest point on the Camino. There is a cross located there that has been a stopping point for hundreds of years. Tradition since ancient times has been to bring a rock from your homeland to place at the foot of the cross at Cruz de Ferro. Before leaving home, we both found small rocks to take with us. I had a small piece of quartz that I found in our yard. I had packed it in my pack and had pretty much forgotten about it until today. We reached the Cruz de Ferro shortly after sunup. There is a small chapel there with benches. It was a beautiful day, and you could see forever in every direction.

The first thing we did was to take off all of the extra layers of clothing we were wearing. We were both soaking wet from sweat. We were the only people at the Cruz de Ferro. I searched through my backpack, found my piece of quartz, and headed up to the cross. Because so many rocks have been placed at the foot of the cross over the last two thousand years, the metal cross has been put onto a large oak pole to elevate it above the rock pile.

As I reached the base of the cross, I was hit by the importance of this event. I had not expected this type of reaction on my part. I think it focused everything from the original idea to do this trip years ago, to all of the planning and preparation, and the many hard miles behind us. As I placed the small rock that I had carried so many miles at the foot of the cross, I had tears in my eyes and was choking back sobs. The small stone also reminded me of home and our daughters. I placed the rock at the base of the cross and leaned against the pole for a moment.

As I walked down from the pile of rocks, Diddo took her turn. When she came down, I could see that the event had the same effect on her. As with so many things on the Camino, this turned out to be much more of a memory than I had expected. As we put our packs back on and walked away from the Cruz del Ferro, we were both quiet, reflecting on our reactions.

The trail was fairly level for a while. We were walking into the morning clouds from the west side of the mountains. The clouds formed a heavy fog that was receding as fast as we approached. There was beauty in every direction. Prior to reaching the abandoned village of Manjarin, Diddo spotted a huge horse standing in the fog. It didn't look real, more like a ghost horse. It was beautiful, spooky, and surreal, all in one.

We reached Manjarin a short time later. The only thing there is an *albergue* run by an eccentric character who claims to be the last of the Templar Knights. It looked to me more like the late sixties in a commune in California. Diddo had a cup of coffee while we took a short break.

From Manjarin we went downhill on the road, then up a steep hill next to a Spanish military base. Signs warned us that we were to keep a distance from the base. It appeared to be a major communications center.

From here on out, it was downhill for the rest of the day, and I mean a long, steep downhill. The trail went along the road, intersected by some dirt trail shortcuts between sections of the road. The dirt sections of the trail were shorter than the road route, but they were very steep, rocky, and rugged. After the second of these sections, which took us into the village of Acebo, we decided to stay on the road the rest of the way into Molinaseca.

We stopped in Acebo at an open bar along with several other pilgrims. We had coffee and an *empanada*. The *empanada* consisted of fried dough filled with pork and onions. It was quite good.

We continued on the long downhill, shunning the dirt trail sections, into the village of Riego. The day had warmed up, and we were both starting to tire out. We passed by the last dirt cut-off and continued on the road. A sheepherder stopped us and, with hand signals, told us that we had missed the dirt trail cut-off. We told him we were going to stick to the road. He shrugged his shoulders in a knowing way that made us wonder if we were making the right decision. The road route was much longer than it looked on the map-narrow, with many hairpin turns. Luckily, there was not much traffic because there was very little room at the side of the road. It seemed to go on and on.

Just when I thought that we were crazy for walking along this section of road, we came around a corner and encountered hikers who were going up the road! I don't think that the folks in Spain worry about getting hit by a car as much as Californians.

Finally, we saw Molinaseca up ahead. We could also see the trail section and the steep downhill the other pilgrims were on. I think we made the right decision.

We were hot, tired, and sore; and it had been a tough and emotional day. We had covered almost seventeen miles over a mountain range. We were hoping beyond hope that the place where we had made our reservation, the Hostal Palacio, was nice.

We walked through the outskirts of town and then crossed a beautiful bridge into the old town. We found our hostel right on the other side of the bridge. We went in, found the manager, and checked in. She took us to our room, gave us the key, and told us to come down and pay after we had rested up. We thanked her and used the key to get into the room.

As soon as we entered the room, we both stopped in our tracks. The room was huge. Windowed doors led out onto a private, enclosed balcony that had a view of the bridge and river. The room was beautiful. Diddo asked me how much the room cost. I told her that I thought it was 42 euros. As I said this, I knew that couldn't be right. This room had to be way more than that. Diddo didn't even take off her pack.

I exited the room and went looking for the manager. I found her down the hallway and asked her again how much the room was. She said in Spanish that the room was 42 euros. I wanted to make sure, so I had her write it down. There it was, in black and white, 42 euros.

We got settled in the room, took showers, and went down to the hostel restaurant to eat. This place didn't follow the Spanish tradition regarding meal times and served meals throughout the day. We had the Menu del Dia: salad, veal filets with fries, and ice cream. Nine and a half euros each for a very good meal.

We went back to the room and washed our clothes. They were very dirty from sweat, grime, and dirt. We both crashed for a while. It had been a long, tough day, and we had several long hard days ahead of us, according to the guidebook.

We went out to find the *albergue* and ran into Bill, who pointed us in the right direction. Unfortunately, the *albergue* was about a mile out of town, so we had a long walk.

The *albergue* was so full that they had tents set up in the yard area to accommodate the overflow. We went inside and asked to have our credentials stamped. The *albergue* manager seemed rather abrupt with us, but he gave us our stamps.

We walked around looking for an open store, with no luck. We went back to the hostel restaurant, had a couple of beers while sitting outside enjoying the evening, then bought some bottled water and croissants at the bar for tomorrow morning.

We headed back to the room and watched Spanish TV. We have a long day tomorrow, over 20 miles. On the map it looked fairly flat, but we will see.

It looked like we were in for warmer weather. We will be going through Ponferrada in the morning. It is the last big city we have to walk through before reaching Santiago. We will be glad to have that behind us.

Camino into Foncebadon

Diddo placing her rock under the cross

Emotional moment at Cruz de Ferro

Horse in the clouds

Retreating clouds

Last of the Templar albergue in Manjarin

Bridge into Molinaseca

View from our room at the Hostal Palacio

CHAPTER 32

September 24, 2003-Wednesday-Day 29
Molinaseca to Villafranca

21 Miles

THERE was a lot of noise around the hostel during the night so we didn't get a full night's sleep. We had the croissants in the room before we took off.

Our plan was to take a shortcut through Ponferrada. We were walking with Bill, and because we were talking and not paying attention, we missed the shortcut turn off. By the time we realized our mistake, it was too late to turn around. We stayed on the main Camino trail which goes right through downtown Ponferrada.

One of the interesting sights in Ponferrada is the Castillo de los Templarios. This impressive 12th Century castle was the Templars' base for the protection of Ponferrada and the surrounding area. It would have been worth a closer look if we didn't have such a long haul today.

The Camino trail was not well marked through the city. Out of frustration, we asked for assistance from an old man with a cane who pointed us in the right direction. As we were walking along the river path, we were stopped by an old woman who told us not to follow the markers. She instructed us to follow the river trail to the main highway, past what appeared to be an old abandoned factory.

We came to an intersection that had yellow arrow trail markings pointing in a different direction than the old woman's instructions. So far, we have had good luck following the yellow arrows, so we disregarded the old woman's advice and followed the yellow arrows. The map, as far as we could tell, also showed the route indicated by the arrows. This turned out to be a good choice.

The trail after this point was very plainly marked. The outskirts of Ponferrada seemed to go on forever. We were very happy when we finally left the city area and reached the countryside. The trail was fairly flat and made for good walking. We ran into Bill outside of the city. He had taken the other route, so I guess both of them worked.

We took a short break after going under a freeway underpass. A woman who was walking by asked us if we were OK. We told her we were just taking a break.

Just prior to Fuentes Nuevas, a group of German high school students passed us. By the look of their gear, they had just started the Camino. There were two older men with them who were leading the group. They all seemed to be having a great time. One of the students was carrying a guitar in a case. I wondered how long it would take for that guitar to become a real burden. We would play trail tag with this group for the next several days. They always seemed to be full of energy; however, the guitar changed hands many times during their trek on the Camino.

When we reached Fuentes Nuevas, a small village a few miles outside of Ponferrada, I saw a bar with an outside menu that advertised *huevos fritos con tostada y bacon*: fried eggs, toast and bacon! This was the first time we had seen eggs, bacon, and toast on a menu. We stopped and went inside. I asked the young woman behind the counter if she really had eggs and toast, and to my surprise the answer was yes. We put in our order.

The woman we had seen earlier came into the bar and asked the same question about the menu. When we heard her speak English, we asked her where she was from, to which she replied "Missouri." She sat down, and we all had a nice talk while we waited for our food. When the food came-two eggs sunny side up, bacon, and toast-we dug in and had a feast. Nothing like home cooking!

We took off refreshed, but the day had warmed up and we could tell that it was only going to get worse. On this stretch, we seemed to go from village to village. We went through the town of Camponaraya, which is built along the main highway. Like most highway towns, it seems to go on forever.

Outside of Camponaraya, the trail left the road for a while and went through a couple of miles of vineyards. This was harvest season, so the vineyards were filled with workers picking the grapes, along with tractors and trailers to haul the grapes. Very busy, very dusty.

After making it through the vineyards, we crossed the main highway and followed the road to Cacabelos. Just outside of Cacabelos there was a small park with a fountain and a covered picnic table area. What a relief. We were very hot and needed a break from the sun. We stopped, ate a snack, and rested for about twenty minutes. I soaked my hat in the ice-cold water to keep cool.

Bill caught up to us at the park. He said that, according to his calculations, Villafranca was just up ahead. I told him I thought it was a ways farther and, unfortunately, I was right.

We also met two French couples who would be with us on and off until Santiago. At first, it seemed like a weird deal. One couple drove a vehicle, a big BMW, from town to town. They would park, then hike back and meet the other couple, who were walking the whole Camino. The couple doing the walking carried very little gear. Most of their stuff was hauled around in the vehicle. We heard other pilgrims complaining about these folks because they sometimes stayed in the *albergue*s, and people did not think that was right. At first glance, I felt the same way; however, after thinking about it, I realized that I did not have all of the facts. Maybe the woman or man had some illness, and this was the only way they could make the trip. They were very nice people, they were doing the Camino, and that was good enough for me.

Maybe other pilgrims talked about us because we stayed in hotels or hostels. I guess if you carried the purist deal all the way, everyone should be penniless, wearing robes, and walking barefoot. Some folks feel that there is a need to suffer if you are going to be a pilgrim. If you were barefoot, wearing long robes, and had no money or food, you could really get into the suffering in a big way. The thing we figured out is that you, and you alone, can do the Camino. If you are going to walk across a strange country for 500 plus miles, in all types of weather, with everything you need on your back, you have to be the one to do it. Rich or poor, you still have to put in the miles. You can have the best boots and best pack that money can buy, but you are still going to have sore legs, sore feet, and a back that is really tired at the end of the day.

Cacabelos was just past the rest stop. It also proved to be a long town to walk through, with lots of activity. Most of our fellow pilgrims were taking a lunch break, but we decided to keep going. We both wanted to get to Villafranca.

Outside of Cacabelos, the trail was just the shoulder of a very busy highway. Between Cacabelos and Villafranca was a very steep uphill, with no relief from the sun. It seemed to go on forever, and we had to stay alert for the cars, trucks, and tractors speeding down the highway.

After a very long, hot, exhausting three miles, we could see Villafranca. It looked like it was just around the corner, on the highway. Just when we thought we were there, the trail turned off the highway and headed through more vineyards. What was worse, this trail started uphill, and I mean really steep uphill. As we were struggling up this grade, a huge semi truck started down the hill. The dirt road was very narrow, with almost no shoulder. We both got as far off the dirt road as we could to let the huge truck get by.

This trail seemed to be never-ending. Diddo was convinced that we were lost, but I kept coming across the yellow arrows, so I was confident that we were on the right path. Just when we were about to give up, we came into the outskirts of Villafranca. We finally reached the *albergue* and decided to get our credentials stamped so that we did not have to come back later. After such a long, hard day, we wanted to do as little walking as possible. This was one of those days when everything hurt, and the idea of doing any extra walking just wasn't in the cards.

We entered the *albergue* and were greeted by the managers. It was cool inside. We sat down, and one of the staff brought us two glasses of water. Very nice folks. They gave us directions to our hotel, the Hotel San Francisco, located on the main plaza.

Villafranca is built on a steep hillside, so everywhere you go is either a steep uphill or downhill. This town could wear you out! We finally found the main plaza and the hotel. We checked in: older place, but clean.

We were beat, hot, tired, and dirty. After long, hot showers that washed the day away, we headed out to eat. We put off the clothes washing until later.

We went down to the plaza where there were several restaurants with outside tables. We picked one and had a couple of cold beers. Boy, did they taste great.

The restaurant had bacon cheeseburgers, so I ordered one with fries. Diddo had the Menu del Dia: salad and fried chicken breast with fries. The food was not very good, which was too bad because we were looking forward to a good meal. The meal was 13 euros for both of us.

We headed back to the room and did the washing. I went out to find a pay phone to make a reservation in O'Cebreiro. O'Cebreiro is one of those places that is at the end of a long haul, with not much else in the area. I found a telephone, but the phone number in our guidebook turned out to be a fax. I looked for a telephone book, but O'Cebreiro is in Galicia, so the Castilla y Leon book did not do me any good.

I went back to the hotel and, using the English/Spanish deal, asked the desk clerk if he had a telephone book that would list O'Cebreiro. He asked me what number I wanted. It turned out that he had the telephone number of the hostel in his address book. He made the call for me and reserved a room, or at least I think he did. There was a little confusion in the translations. I paid the desk clerk for the long distance charge and thanked him.

We crashed in the room for a while and then went out to check on the trail out of town and get supplies.

There are two trail options when leaving Villafranca. One goes along the road. The other route goes up on a high hillside, through the forest for a couple of miles, then rejoins the road route. The second route is supposed to be a nice forest trail, with a hard climb at the start. It was going to be dark for the first couple of hours that we were on the trail, so we decided to take the shorter road route. Scenery is no good if you can't see it. We found the split just before the trail left town.

We ran into Buddy and Estelle, who were also researching the trail. We had seen them in the Plaza at lunch, which was a big surprise. We had not seen them since before Viana. Estelle had heat stroke and had to take a few days off. They were still plugging along, and both looked good.

On the way back to the hotel, we stopped at a couple of stores and got hand cream, shampoo for clothes washing, bread, bananas, Dove soap, bottled water, and candy.

Diddo was hungry, so we stopped at a restaurant and had some soup and bread. We ran into Jean Pierre, the guy we met on the bus bench outside of Astorga. He looked better and was still going strong. He said that he finally walked into Astorga after we left the bus bench. He took a cab from Astorga to Foncebadon but had been walking ever since. He was still having shin splint problems.

We went to the room to get our gear ready. Tomorrow should be one of the last big days. We would be going over the last big mountain range. The map showed a mega climb that looked like a real butt kicker. The distance is about twenty miles. We were looking forward to getting this section behind us.

We have had several long hard days, with several more to come. Today was a real tough one. Not flat, as we had thought. It was hot, dusty, and hard work. Other than having sore feet and being a little tired, we were both still good to go.

Castillo de los Templarios-Ponferrada

Villafranca-end of a long day

CHAPTER 33

September 25, 2003-Thursday-Day 30
Villafranca to O'Cebreiro

19 Miles

THIS is a big day. On the trail, you hear a lot about this section of the Camino and how tough it is supposed to be.

We were up early and away by 6:30 a.m. It was very cold but as clear as a bell. We went through the streets of Villafranca to the point where the trail divided and took the road/river route. The trail markings were easy to follow, even in the dark.

The guidebook says the trail goes along the road, so we were a little concerned about traffic. When we reached the road trail, we found that the trail does go along the road, but there is a cement barrier between the traffic lanes and the trail. The road parallels the Autopista and appears to be the old road.

Even though it was dark, we could still tell that the surrounding area was beautiful. We walked next to the river for about 5.5 miles. The trail was great, and easy walking. Because we were in a deep river valley, it was very cold.

As the sun was coming up, we reached the village of Trabadelo. We were both in need of a hot cup of coffee and something to eat. There was a bar/café on the road just off the trail. We had coffee and a *tortilla* that really hit the spot.

The sun was up when we got back onto the trail, but it was still very cold. The trail stayed on the road, but still had its own lane. The river was never far away as we continued on to La Portela de Valcarce. We made a quick pit stop at the hostel/truck stop.

Just outside of La Portela de Valcarce, there was a pilgrim monument with the mileage listed to Santiago, 190 kilometers, or 118 miles. The trail was a steady but slight, uphill. At Ruitelan, however, this changed dramatically.

We were away from the Autopista on a country road. The grade started to get steeper and steeper. After Herrerias, it was no more mister nice guy.

We could see the top of the mountains and at times could make out buildings along the ridge. We hoped beyond hope that they were not O'Cebreiro, but we knew in our hearts that they were.

About a mile outside of Herrerias, the trail went off-road. There was a marker directing bicycles to stay on the road and walkers to go on the trail. The trail, unfortunately, went downhill for a distance. At the bottom of this short downhill we started up a very steep, rocky, and rough uphill that seemed never-ending.

We took one short break to catch our breath. Two German men whom we had been leapfrogging since Ruitelan caught up and passed us. We took off and caught up to them just before the small village of La Faba. There was a split in the trail, and the German in the lead missed the yellow arrow trail marker and headed the wrong way. I hollered at them and pointed out the right path.

We met up again in a bar in La Faba where we all stopped for a short break and something to eat. We had a cheese *bocadillo*, on which we put some of our canned red peppers, which turned out to be a good combination. Diddo had some type of orange drink in a can that she fell in love with. Unfortunately, they only had one can.

The trail followed the road for a very short distance, then went off-road and straight up. This turned into a real grind. The landscape was high pasture, and there was not a flat spot in sight. The animals that graze on these pastures must be lopsided. They were as steep as a ski slope. When we stopped and looked around, the world seemed to fall away in every direction.

We caught up to the Germans, who were sitting with Bill in the very small village of Laguna de Castilla. They were all taking a break at the *albergue*. Bill said that he had missed the trail marker and continued on the road. I think that might have been a good mistake because he had been behind us and had made good time on the road.

We had a good rhythm going, so we decided to keep on truckin'. Up, up, and up. We reached the marker for the border of Galicia and stopped to take a photo. The Germans caught up to us, both of them breathing hard. One of them told me in broken English that O'Cebreiro was about 15 or 50 minutes away. I couldn't understand which one he was saying. I couldn't imagine that it was 50 minutes, so I was hoping he meant 15 minutes.

Diddo and I took off, determined that our next stop would be O'Cebreiro. About fifteen minutes from the marker, we came around a bend and there was the village of O'Cebreiro. It was such a great feeling to finally reach the top of the mountain. When we stopped and looked back, we couldn't comprehend how we could have made the climb. It almost gave us vertigo because we seemed to be on top of the world.

This had been a tough day, on top of several tough days. It was a great feeling to know we had made it to this point.

Our arrival time was three o'clock. We were beat, but felt good that this section of trail was behind us. We used the last of our energy to find the hostel, where, we hoped we had a reservation. We entered just as they were serving the afternoon meal. The dining room was packed. O'Cebreiro is quite a tourist destination. There were tour buses and cars parked everywhere. We finally got the attention of the owner/manager. He apologized and asked if we could wait for about ten minutes. We grabbed a seat.

An English guy who was sitting nearby eating soup told us that we were at the wrong place. He said that the place we wanted was on the other side of the village. I was confused at first and re-checked to see if we were at the right hostel. He continued to tell us that we were in the wrong place. I finally figured out that he thought we were looking for the *albergue*. His attitude kind of pissed me off, so I told him that we were in the right place, then ignored him.

The manager got the meals served and then took us to our room. Great room, very clean, modern, and nice. There was a TV, but it only received one channel.

We wanted to get some pictures before it got dark, so we took showers, good long, hot showers, washed clothes, and headed over to the *albergue* to get our credentials stamped. We walked around the village, took photos, and just enjoyed O'Cebreiro.

O'Cebreiro is the gateway into Galicia. This area of Spain is noted for its Celtic background. Several of the Celtic-style, round, stonewalled, thatched-roofed buildings still stand in O'Cebreiro and the rest of Galicia. It is not uncommon for Galicians to have red hair and blue eyes. Most of the people in this area speak Galician, along with Spanish. Galician music has a strong Irish sound. It almost felt like we were in Ireland.

O'Cebreiro was also the home of Don Elias Valina Sampedro, the parish priest who devoted his life to restoring the Camino de Santiago. A bust of this remarkable man, who passed away in 1990, stands outside of the Hostal San Giraldo de Aurillac, where we were staying. We learned later that his family still owns and operates the hostel.

We went to the hostel restaurant and paid for the room, 46 euros. I called and made a reservation for a place in Triacastela, our destination for tomorrow. The owner's father gave us the name of the place and said it was the only hostel in Triacastela with bathrooms in the rooms.

After kicking back in the room for a while, we went back out to walk around and do a little shopping. It was starting to get very cold.

We went to the hostel restaurant for dinner. As usual, they didn't start serving dinner until eight o'clock. We were starved by that time.

While we were waiting for dinner, we talked to the British guy we had met earlier. He said that he started the Camino with a plan to complete it in 27 days. He said that he had been doing great until yesterday when he started having a bad pain in the heel of his foot. He went on to say that he could barely walk and thought that he was going to have to quit and go home. This must really be hard when you are this close to the end. He said that he was going to rest his feet for a couple of days, then give it another try. He was not holding out much hope.

It seemed that a lot of the pilgrims who started out with a rigid schedule had this kind of problem. The time limits they set for themselves caused them to push harder than their bodies could take. I am glad that we started slow, then worked up to the higher mileage. It seems to be getting us through, but we are not there yet, so I will withhold my judgment.

We had the Menu del Dia: salad, pork chops with fries, and flan. Everything was very good. Seventeen euros for both of us.

When we arrived in O'Cebreiro, the trail dead-ended into a paved road. I assumed that this was the road that we would take out of town the next morning. Looking at the map, I became a little confused. We noticed that there was another paved road on the other side of the village. Luckily for us, we asked and found that the other road was the one we wanted. The first road would have taken us in the wrong direction. We were both glad that we checked and didn't go with our first impression.

We headed to the room, watched the one channel on TV, and got things ready for tomorrow. I started to write in my journal, but got the hand cramps I had back in Roncesvalles. It got so bad that I couldn't write. I still think that it is from using the walking stick over an extended period of time. The cramps started in my wrist area then went into the fingers.

We were both very tired and hit the sack early. We didn't have to get an early start in the morning. Our plan was to leave about 7:30 or 8:00. It looked like mostly downhill to Triacastela. We were expecting cold weather, hoping for no rain.

Early morning out of Villafranca on the road trail

Statue of St. James-La Portela de Valcarce

Mileage guide at base of statue

Camino along a country road

Vega de Valcarce

Castillo Saracin

Herrerias

Camino traffic jam

Long uphill into La Faba

View up to O'Cebreiro

View back down the valley

Border marker for Galicia

Last few steps before O'Cebreiro

View from O'Cebreiro

View from O'Cebreiro

Hostal San Giraldo de Aurillac-O'Cebreiro

Main street-O'Cebreiro

Gallic construction

CHAPTER 34

September 26, 2003-Friday-Day 31
O'Cebreiro to Triacastela

13 Miles

WE didn't set any alarm for this morning, and we both slept like rocks. It was very cold last night, so we put on extra layers of clothing, expecting cold for the first part of the hike.

We took off, saying goodbye to O'Cebreiro at about 7:45 a.m. I knew that we still had a lot of trail in front of us but, for the first time, I felt that we were on the downhill side of the Camino.

It was still dark when we left, but the trail went right along the road, making it easy to follow. There was hardly any traffic, so it was easy going. It turned out to be much warmer that we expected, so we stopped at the first little village and shed the extra layers of clothing. We took off just as the sun was coming up. The view from the mountain ridge was spectacular.

There were a lot of pilgrims on the trail. The closer we have gotten to Santiago, the more crowded the trail has become. Many of the pilgrims are doing just the last sixty or so miles of the trail. To obtain the Compostela, a pilgrim must complete the last one hundred kilometers (62 miles) of the Camino. From here on out, we expected to see a lot of new faces.

Even though we were on the downside of the Camino, there were still a few hills in front of us. The first climb of the day led to a high point where there is a very impressive pilgrim's monument, a large bronze statue of Santiago, facing into the wind as he walks through the pass. I knew just how he felt, because it was very windy as we made our way through this area.

The trail stayed with the road until just outside of Padornelo. The last climb of the day started here and led to Alto do Poio, the highest point of the Camino in Galicia. We had a choice of staying on the road or going through the village of Padornelo on a side trail. Since the Padornelo route went downhill and we knew we would have to go back uphill, we stayed on the road route. I hate giving up hard-earned altitude. Most of the other pilgrims seemed to be of the same mind.

After a long, hard climb we reached Alto do Poio. There were two bars at this high point, and everyone stopped for coffee and something to eat. There was only one young woman working at the place, and she didn't seem very interested. We waited forever, as did everyone else, but finally got our coffee. I would have liked something to eat, but we didn't have that much time. We had the coffee and some of the little donuts we carried in our packs.

We took off, still going along the road. Diddo had shin splints, and the long downhill seemed to make them worse.

We went through a couple of small villages, each of which had dairy cows being herded through the streets. The streets in these villages were covered with cow droppings, and flies seemed to cover everything. These villages appeared to be very poor, with the women doing most of the work. Although the villages weren't very appealing, the countryside was beyond beautiful.

When we reached the village of Biduedo we took a short break at a little coffee shop. It is about four miles from Biduedo to Triacastela, and it is all downhill, very steep downhill. I was a little worried about Diddo's shin splints, but she wasn't complaining, so we kept on truckin'.

At one point, we could see Triacastela way down in the valley. The trail was great, but the long downhill really started to punish our legs. After going through several more small villages, cattle and flies included, we reached the valley floor. It was a great feeling to be walking on flat ground.

When we reached Triacastela we stopped at the *albergue* to get our credentials stamped. The *albergue* was built inside an old school. Apparently this is quite common in Galicia. The *albergue* was very nice and looked like it had a lot of room.

We continued on into town and found the Meson Vilasante. We checked in at the bar, and, after confirming our reservation, the woman running the place took us to our room on the third floor, up the steepest staircase I have ever seen. The room was a little run down, but it may be the best place in Triacastela. The room cost 35 euros.

Taking a shower was a real adventure. The water went from very hot to very cold without much warning. When Diddo was taking a shower, I heard her yell something. I thought that she was yelling, "My neck, my neck." I jumped up and ran into the bathroom, thinking that she had fallen and hurt herself. When I reached the bathroom, I realized that she was saying, "My necklace, my necklace." Her necklace had broken and the pendant, a small gold dachshund, had disappeared. I put my hand over the drain, then fished around in the water. Luckily I found the pendant before it went down the drain.

We had the Menu del Dia in the *meson* dining room. It consisted of a very hearty potato and spinach soup, beefsteak with fries, wine, and ice cream. Everything was very good, with a price tag of 14 euros for both of us.

We walked around town and checked out the trail for tomorrow morning. There are two routes out of Triacastela. One of the routes goes via Samos to Sarria. The other trail is a more direct route to Sarria. We decided to take the more direct, shorter route, even though it is hillier.

We headed to the room and washed our clothes, then crashed for a while. We went back out to get supplies, candy, something to eat in the morning, mints, and bottled water. I bought some playing cards so I could play solitaire.

We went back over the route out of town because it was a little confusing and, we knew it was going to be a challenge in the dark. It was getting cloudy and cold, and it looked like rain for tomorrow.

Diddo wanted a glass of wine, so we stopped at a little bar up the street from our *meson*. I just had a glass of water. We watched TV there for a while and just kicked back. The bartender was a young woman who had her little daughter with her while she worked. There were three guys at the bar, one of whom was a loud mouth. He kept trying to grab the bartender every time she walked by. She played it off well, but I could see that she was getting real tired of this drunk.

Having spent a good part of my life dealing with guys like this, I knew that the situation could go from bad to worse at any time, and I didn't want to be around when it did.

At one point the drunk accidentally knocked over his glass, which broke on the floor behind the bar. The other guys with the drunk were telling him to tone it down, but we all know how much good that does.

When Diddo finished her wine, we paid our bill and took off. I was glad to get out of the place, but couldn't help feeling sorry for the bartender, who was trying to make a living, and had to put up with that kind of crap.

We got back to the room, took off our boots, and started getting ready for tomorrow. I took the insoles out of my boots to air them out and had just started to make a minor repair on the shoulder strap of my backpack. Diddo was doing something when it suddenly occurred to her that she didn't have her purse. Panic hit both of us. Everything was in her purse: plane tickets, money, her passport, our credentials, credit cards, everything. She never, never let it out of her sight. She said she knew she had it at the bar. I put on by boots, sans insoles, and didn't even stop to lace them up. I flew down the three flights of steep steps, out to the street, and ran the one block to the bar. There must not be much running in Triacastela because everyone was looking at me. I ran into the bar, and before I could even ask the question, the bartender handed me the purse. What a relief. I couldn't thank her enough. I stepped out into the street and could see Diddo hanging out of the window, looking up the street. I gave her the thumbs up and, even from a block away, could see the relief on her face.

I had left the room in such a hurry I didn't have any money. I thanked the young woman again and headed back to the room where I reunited Diddo with her purse. I put the insoles back into my boots, laced them up, grabbed a five euro note, and walked back to the bar. When I gave the bartender the five euro bill, she said in Spanish that it was not necessary. I insisted that she take it and thanked her again.

Both of us were shaken by this event. We couldn't help but play the "what if" game, just as when I fell down outside of Estella. After a few minutes though, we put it behind us.

Good hike today. Both of us had some aches and pains, not so much from just today, but the combination of the last several days. They have been long, hard, high-mileage days. The miles are starting to have an effect on our bodies. God willing, in six more days, we will be in Santiago. We don't want anything to give out on us now!

Tomorrow is about 11 or so miles to Sarria. We tried to get reservations at the Alfonso IX, a three-star hotel, but they said that they were full. We did make a reservation at a hostel. We are hoping that the good weather holds, but it looks like rain.

Pilgrim's monument

View toward Padornelo and Alto do Poio

View from the Camino

Busy café at Alto do Poio

Triacastela

CHAPTER 35

September 27, 2003-Saturday-Day 32
Triacastela to Sarria

11 Miles

WE didn't get any sleep last night. It was very noisy outside, and also inside the *meson*. The walls were thin, and there was a lot of coming and going. It was also very cold. There wasn't any heat in the room, and not much in the way of insulation. To top things off, there wasn't any hot water in the morning.

When we hit the trail, it was still cold and dark outside. Once we got going, we warmed up.

The trail went along a paved country road for a while. We went by a warehouse that had three very loud, barking, mean-looking dogs on long chains. They went after anyone or anything that went by the place.

A short distance later, the trail went off-road up a steep hill into the small village of A Balsa. It was still dark, and it did not appear that the village had many inhabitants. It was the same story as yesterday with the cows and their droppings. Everything was very wet, which seemed to add to the bad smell. These villages start to get a little depressing after a while.

The trail became very steep and difficult to walk up because there was so much mud. It must have rained last night. The trail hit the road again, but the grade continued to be very steep.

About the time the sun came up, we reached a short but welcome level area by the small village of San Xil. There was one more uphill, then we started down, down, down. Walking on pavement down these steep grades was very hard on our legs.

I started having a pain in my right heel/Achilles tendon that I think was from the long uphill climbs we had been doing the last few days. At this stage of the game, I had become a little paranoid about the aches and pains we were having. We were so close that we didn't want anything to prevent us from reaching Santiago.

We went through a few villages, but there was nothing in the way of bars or cafes. In one small village, we saw an old woman herding cows with a younger man. She looked least a hundred years old. There were lots of pilgrims on the trail. It looked like most of the people decided to take this route.

We finally found an open bar in Furela. It was good timing, because I was running out of gas. We had toast with butter and jam and coffee. We both felt much better after the break.

As we continued, the trail had some up and downs, but nothing difficult. Every village we went through seemed to have a lot of dogs that did not like pilgrims. There were also a lot of cattle and sheep on the trail. The weather turned out great. It was cool, but nice for hiking.

We thought that when we reached Sarria we would try again at the Alfonso IX. After last night, we could really use a nice room and a good night's sleep.

We got to Sarria about 12:30 p.m. The Alfonso IX turned out to be located on the near side of town, just before the bridge crossing into Sarria. It looked like a great hotel. We went in and asked at the desk if they had any rooms. The desk clerk checked and gave us an affirmative reply. We checked in and headed to the room. The bill was 51 euros, and it looked like it was worth every cent. The room turned out to be just like the rest of the hotel, fantastic. The Alfonso IX is a NH Hotel, like the one we stayed at in Logrono.

We did our wash, then took long, hot bath/showers to make up for yesterday. I soaked my feet and felt like a new man.

We went to the hotel restaurant to eat. We ordered off the menu, no Menu del Dia in this place. I had a big thick juicy steak with fries, the best one so far.

We devoured every bite of our food. It came to 48 euros. I know that I have said this before, but it was worth every cent. The price included a bottle of wine and bottled water. What a difference a good room, being clean, and a great meal makes.

We crashed in the room for a couple of hours, then walked around town. We took the trail to the edge of town, then stopped at the *albergue* and had our credentials stamped. We ran into Bill and Jean Pierre. Jean Pierre said that his shin splints were getting better, and he thought he would make it all the way. Bill said that he was going to do some long days because he was getting short on time. This was the last time we saw him. We heard later that he made it into Santiago a couple of days ahead of us.

We walked around town and picked up some supplies. We made a quick stop at the ATM for some cash before heading back to the hotel. We made reservations at a hotel that is part of the Spanish Parador chain in Portomarin for the next night. We had decided that these last few days we would stay in the best hotels we could find, kind of a reward for all of the hard work.

Camino trail-Sarria in the distance

Sarria

CHAPTER 36

September 28, 2003-Sunday-Day 33
Sarria to Portomarin

14 Miles

I slept like a rock. There was a big wedding reception at the hotel that went on most of the night, but the party didn't keep us awake. It looked like everyone in Sarria was at the bash. In the morning we ate rolls in the room before heading out at about 7:00 a.m. It was very dark once we left town, but the route was clearly marked and easy to follow.

There was a long unexpected uphill right out of town. The morning was cool, perfect for hiking. The countryside on this section of the Camino was beautiful. The villages we went through were cleaner and better kept than the villages we had seen in the last couple of days.

Diddo had a calf muscle cramp that I thought might be a problem, but she walked it off. It seemed that at this point in the journey, everything hurt at some time during the day. I felt that our minds and bodies were getting tired of the trail. Even though we tried not to think about it, the end was just a few days away. It was hard not to think about Santiago and heading home. We didn't want to get ahead of ourselves. We had to keep our minds on today.

We finished the long uphill just as the sun was coming up. The terrain flattened out which made for easier walking. It stayed this way most of the rest of the day until just outside of Portomarin.

The countryside was beautiful. The villages had nice homes, and everything appeared to be very well maintained. We stopped at a little café just off the trail in Ferrerios for toast with butter and jam, and some coffee.

The clouds were at ground level just like fog. It started to mist hard enough that we stopped and put on our rain gear. The mist made for great hiking. Rock walls covered with moss, lots of green vegetation, it must be like this most of the time.

We reached the 100-kilometer marker to Santiago. This is a big event, so we stopped and took photos. After reaching a high ridge, we started a long, long, downhill. We stopped once just to take the packs off and rest.

As we descended we got out of the clouds, so we shed the rain gear. The last mile or so was downhill on a very steep, paved road that was very hard on the legs. After reaching the valley, we came to a monster bridge that crosses the lake at Portomarin. The lake was very low, making the bridge appear even more ominous. This thing is over a half mile long, and as we were crossing it really took our breath away.

Portomarin is built on a high bluff above the lake, so when we reached the other side of the bridge we still had a long uphill grade into town. We reached the main intersection where the *albergue* is located. We asked directions to the Pousada de Portomarin, a three-star hotel that is part of the Spanish government's Parador system. Turned out it was right down the street.

We checked into the hotel and headed to our room. We were both a little disappointed. The price of the place was not cheap, 75 euros, and it was not up to par with other places we had stayed at in that price range. The hotel itself was well-kept, but the room needed maintenance.

We soaked our feet and took showers, then headed down to the hotel restaurant. We became concerned because we were the only people in the large dining room. We decided to split a meal. We ordered a salad, an order of spaghetti with shrimp and mushrooms, and a filet mignon dinner with fries. Everything was fantastic! The salad was more than enough for two people. The spaghetti really hit the spot. The filet mignon was two medallions that were out of this world. Dessert was the best ice cream sundae I ever had. Vanilla and walnut ice cream, chocolate sauce, wow!

Looking at my notes, I see that I talk a lot about food. I think that it becomes such a pleasure at the end of a long day of hiking that it really makes an impression.

At about 6:00, we went out. We stopped at the *albergue* and had our credentials stamped. The *albergue* looked like it was way overcrowded. The increase in the number of pilgrims the last one hundred kilometers really overloads the system.

We walked the route out of town. The trail went back across the lake over a footbridge that is built on top of a large steel water pipe. It looked scary. There is an alternate road bridge route just about a quarter mile farther. They both wind up at the same place. I planned on taking the road bridge.

After a couple of beers at a bar in town, we packed it in for the night. Today was a great day on the Camino. We have a long day tomorrow, I think about seventeen miles or so.

Misty morning out of Sarria

View from the Camino

Great trail

100 kilometer marker

Moss covered walls

Main bridge into Portomarin

Portomarin albergue

CHAPTER 37

September 29, 2003-Monday-Day 34
Portomarin to Palas de Rei

17 Miles

WE were on the trail at 6:45 a.m. Not only was it dark, it was also foggy. We made our way down the steep hill that led out of the town to the scary footbridge we had seen from a distance yesterday. Diddo wanted to cross the footbridge because the yellow arrows pointed that way. Diddo hates bridges, so this really freaked me out. I told her in no uncertain terms that I wanted to use the road bridge. As usual, her no uncertain terms beat my no uncertain terms, so we started across the footbridge. As I said before, the footbridge is built on top of a water pipe. It is narrow, has very low railings, and the whole thing shook as we walked across it. It was pitch black, but we knew that the water and rocks were a long, long drop below us. Crossing this bridge scared the heck out of me. I had to concentrate on my feet or else I was afraid that I would freeze up. I even had this weird feeling that I was being pulled down. I could feel my breathing quicken with fright. The bridge is several hundred feet long, and it seemed to take forever to get across. When we reached the other side, it was a great relief. I was mad at Diddo, and told her that I wouldn't ever do that again. Diddo didn't say much, so I think that she was a little shook up also.

Later, when we were talking about it and I told her that I had this weird feeling that I was being pulled down, she started to laugh. I asked her what was so funny. She explained that she was so scared that she grabbed onto the back of my backpack and held on for dear life all the way across the bridge. We both had a good laugh about that.

We found the trail on the other side of the bridge with no problem. The trail in this area appeared to be well marked, and very well maintained. I think that this will be the case the rest of the way into Santiago because it is so heavily traveled.

After a long, steady uphill, we reached a plateau about sunup. We thought that we were almost alone on the trail, until we took a look behind us and saw a parade of pilgrims.

The trail went along next to the main highway for six miles or so. We made one quick stop for some coffee at the first bar we found open. It was great walking this morning, cool, and foggy. We were making great time, and really enjoying this section of the Camino.

At the small village of Hospital, the trail went over the main highway and continued on a narrow paved country road. The fog was very heavy as we approached the high point of today's hike at Sierra Ligonde. I couldn't see very far off the road, but what I could see was beautiful. When we did reach the high point, the fog was so thick that I started to think that we were the only people on the face of the earth. It was so quiet, peaceful, and beautiful.

We finally started on a downhill grade toward Palas de Rei. For once, it wasn't the usual steep leg killer, just a steady, gradual downhill.

We were starting to get hungry, but passed by a café where a lot of the pilgrims had stopped for a break. We probably should have stopped, because by the time we reached the village of Portos we were starved. We came around a corner, and there was a little bar/café. There were no other customers, but it looked like a nice place. The owner was behind the bar watching a Mexican movie. We ordered calamari with mushrooms and a *tortilla*. Everything was great, and the bill was only five euros. We left full and refreshed. The owner told us that Palas de Rei was just a short distance away and that there were no big hills in between.

The sun broke through the fog just before we reached Palas de Rei. Diddo was beat for some reason and really wanted to get to the end of the trail. I was beginning to wonder where the town was. We passed a very large sport's complex that looked like a first-class operation, then came around a corner and there was the town of Palas de Rei. It is a good-sized town located on the main highway. We reached Palas de Rei at about 1:30.

We had covered almost 17 miles in a little under 7 hours. Great trail, great hiking, one of the best days for me so far.

The hostel we were staying at was right up the main street from the *albergue*. We checked in at the bar as usual and then headed up to the room. It was a nice room, but it may be a little noisy because it overlooks the main street. The room was 36 euros.

After our usual clean-up routine, we headed over to the *albergue* and had our credentials stamped. We had a good meal at the hostel restaurant, then headed up to the room and conked out for a while. We both seem to be tired at the end of each day at this point of the trek. I can feel my body wearing down, but we are getting close.

Later that evening, we went out and picked up some needed supplies, then headed back to the room to catch our favorite Spanish soap opera.

Tomorrow should be the last of several long days in a row. At this point, it is hard not to think of reaching Santiago.

CHAPTER 38

September 30, 2003-Tuesday-Day 35
Palas de Rei to Arzua

18 Miles

WE were getting so close to the end that I couldn't help but think of home. We had a long haul ahead of us, but I thought that this might be the last of the long days. It is about eighteen miles to Arzua, with lots of hills.

We were away at 6:25 a.m. It was cool and very cloudy. The trail was well marked and easy to follow. We were not very far out of town when it started to rain. The rain caught us by surprise; for once, we weren't expecting it. We stopped and put on our rain gear and continued on. The rain was steady, and it looked like it might be with us the rest of the day.

At times during the trip, the pack strap on my right shoulder bugged me. I think that's because of an old neck/shoulder injury. Sometimes the strap hits a nerve and causes me a lot of pain. Today was one of those days. I didn't want to stop and take everything off to adjust the strap in the rain, so we just kept walking.

A little further on, we found a small bar and stopped for coffee and some coffee cake. This was the first place that I had seen since starting the Camino where they use a coffee pot instead of going through the whole single cup espresso deal. This stop gave me a chance to readjust my pack, so when we hit the trail the pack felt a little bit better.

At about 11:30 a.m., we stopped and took a short break at a little picnic area on the trail. I was still having a problem with my pack, so I attempted another readjustment before we took off.

We reached the town of Melide a short time later. Melide turned out to be a pretty good-sized, very busy place. The trail was not well marked and very confusing as it went through town. First it went down back alleys, then out onto the main drag, then back to the alleys. At the main plaza, we completely lost the trail. The best thing to do when this happens is to stop where you are and look around. We followed this tactic, and a minute later Diddo spotted the trail marker and we got back on track.

As we were leaving town, the rain was really coming down. On the west side of Melide we passed a fountain that filled a large cement basin where the local women do their washing. Several women were doing their laundry. This is one of those scenes in Spain that seems so odd. Spain is a very modern country. We had just walked through a large, modern, busy town, and here were folks doing the laundry, outside, at a communal washing area as they have for centuries.

About three miles past Melide, we stopped at a coffee shop in Boente and had a *tortilla con queso*. Basically, it was a cheese omelet. Several of the other pilgrims we had seen along the trail were also there taking a break. I think that everyone just wanted to get out of the rain for a while. We didn't stay long though because it was about five long, hard miles to Arzua. We weren't getting any closer sitting in the bar.

The trail went on a long downhill run, followed by a long uphill to a high ridge. The ridgeline was covered by thick eucalyptus forest. From the ridge, we headed back downhill to a valley. After crossing the valley, it was back uphill to another ridge. Each time we reached a ridge, I was hoping to see Arzua up ahead, but no such luck. One more valley and one more long uphill. The trail was great, but we were both beat.

We started down from the last ridge on a long, very steep downhill into Ribadiso. There was a great-looking *albergue* in Ribadiso that we were tempted to stop at for the night, but our plan called for us to make the extra mileage into Arzua, so we kept on going.

Arzua was only about two miles farther, but unfortunately, it was all uphill. We continued on a killer uphill along the road toward Arzua. Toward the top of the climb, we met two women from Florida. It was nice to stop and talk to them and a great excuse to take a short break and catch our breath. They were doing the last part of the Camino, from Triacastela. It was always great to talk to someone from home.

We started back up the hill and finally reached Arzua. It looked like a long highway town. The place we were staying turned out to be located on the east side of town. It didn't look that great, but it was the only place listed in our guidebook. As usual, the hostel rooms were above a bar. We went into the bar, checked in, and headed to the room. The place was OK, but not the Ritz. It cost 33 euros.

Our idea of staying in top of the line hotels for the last few days had fallen apart, because there weren't any top of the line hotels.

We went through our routine before heading downstairs to see if we could get something to eat. They were not serving any food until eight o'clock.

I used the pay phone in the bar to try to make a reservation at the Parador in Santiago (two days away), but they were full. While I had them on the line, I asked them what the next best hotel was, and they directed me to the five-star Palace de Carmen. I called the Palace de Carmen and made a reservation.

We then tried to get a reservation at the only hotel in Arca, our next planned stop. Everything in Arca was booked full. We were getting so close to Santiago that rooms were getting harder and harder to find.

We went into the restaurant, had a couple of beers, and discussed our options. We were both tired of places like we were staying in tonight, but there was not much else ahead of us. We went over the map and guidebook and decided to make a long haul the following day into Labacolla. It seemed like every time we thought we had made our last long haul, we wound up with one more.

Labacolla is just outside of Santiago. It is where the Santiago airport is located. The more we talked, the better the plan felt. We decided to get away early, haul ass, and try to reach Labacolla, about 18.5 miles.

From there, we could go over to the airport and check on flights to Madrid and home. We were looking forward to two short, relaxing days into Santiago, but that was not going to happen. We were going to have one long day, then one very short day.

We both liked the plan. I called and made a reservation at the Hostal San Paio in Labacolla because it was listed in our guidebook. It didn't say much about the place, but because Labacolla is an airport town, there were several other hotels. We could look around town if we didn't like the Hostal San Paio.

We headed up to the room, washed clothes, and crashed for a while. We were both beat because of the long day and the rain. We were hoping for a dry day tomorrow, but it didn't look good. This area of Spain is famous for rain this time of year.

When we started the Camino, the idea of walking all day in the rain really bothered us. Those first days really kicked our butts. It seems funny to us at this point that we ever considered taking a bus or taxi to avoid the rain. It's not that we like going out in the rain and mud, because it does really wear us out, but it is just not that big of a deal to us anymore.

We had some time to kill, so we walked into town, but there was not much to see. There was a *pension* in the center of town that looked like it might be nicer then our place, but not much else.

Even though it was very cold, windy, and raining, we did check the trail out of town because our guidebook warned that the trail was not well marked and was confusing.

We headed back to the hostel in time to eat. I had soup and bacon and eggs. Diddo had soup and salad. It cost 14 euros for both of us including wine.

Unexpected long day tomorrow. We will see how it goes. The Camino keeps us guessing right to the end.

Bridge into Furelos just outside of Melide

Tree lined Camino

CHAPTER 39

October 1, 2003-Wednesday-Day 36
Arzua to Labacolla

18.5 Miles

WE did not have a good night. The room was very cold, and there was no heater of any type. When we did fall asleep, the hard rain beating on the roof woke us up. I was awake at 4:30, but dozed until the alarm went off at 5:30. Because it was raining so hard outside, we did our rain preparation before leaving the hostel-pack covers, ponchos, and important papers in plastic bags, the whole nine yards.

Diddo was worried about the trail out of town because the guidebook said it was confusing. It turned out to be a piece of cake. The trail was good, but very muddy, and running with water because of the rain. There was hardly anyone else on the trail, probably because of the heavy rain. It is hard to leave a dry, warm room and head out into a storm.

Today was one of those days when my pack was killing my shoulder. I finally stopped, took everything off, and readjusted the straps. It felt much better afterwards.

We were walking through very thick eucalyptus forest with lots of ferns and ground cover. It looked like rain forest, maybe what you would encounter in the northwest United States.

At about 9:00 a.m., we stopped in the small village of Calle. It was the first place where there was anything open. The rain had let up a little, but it was still nice to get inside and have a hot cup of coffee and a little something to eat. Jean Pierre was in the café. He said that his legs were doing much better, and it looked like he was going to make it.

After some fairly flat terrain we came to a long uphill grade toward Santa Irene. At first we were going through farmland and small villages. Before Santa Irene, the trail connected back up to the main highway. The trail crossed and re-crossed the busy highway several times. Each crossing was an adventure because of the heavy traffic and the wet weather.

We reached Santa Irene, the high point of today's section. The trail then headed back across the busy highway and through more eucalyptus forest as it wound its way downhill toward Arca.

Just before reaching Arca, there was a rest area on the highway that had covered tables. We stopped there for a few minutes to take a break. The French couple with the BMW support vehicle was also there. We talked to them for a short time, wished them well, then took off. This was the last time we encountered them.

We were really hoping for a bar or restaurant in Arca. We arrived there at about eleven o'clock, but didn't find anything open, at least not near the trail. We were too beat to explore the town, so we decided to keep going and look for something down the trail.

After crossing and re-crossing the highway a couple more times, we were back into the eucalyptus forest on a very muddy trail heading uphill.

We had covered about 12 miles or so. I guess because we didn't sleep well last night, we were both beat. We were very hungry and needed a break from the weather.

When we reached San Anton, we found a small bar just across the street from a large sport's complex. The woman who was working there was not a real ball of fire, so it was a good thing the place was not busy. I wasn't going to complain about the slow service though, because I wasn't in a big hurry to get back outside into the rain. We had a cheese and egg *tortilla bocadillo* that we split, and one of Diddo's favorite orange drinks.

It was a refreshing break, but when we headed back out it was raining even harder. The only difference now was that there was also thunder and lightning. The funny thing about this storm was that it didn't seem to move. It just stayed right over our heads and dumped rain on us.

Several mountain bikers who were just in front of us decided to pack it in and take cover. It didn't look like it was going to get any better, so we decided to keep on going. The only other people we saw for quite a while were a woman and her son. They were having a really tough time because they didn't have any rain gear.

We crossed the highway one more time, then started up a long, steep grade that led to the high plateau where the airport is located. It was raining so hard that the water was running down the trail like a river. All we could do was slosh through it, stop every few steps and kick the mud off our boots, then take off again. I kept thinking about a long hot shower and a good hot meal. I think that is what kept us going.

We finally reached the top of the mesa where the airport is located. When we were in the forest, it provided a little bit of cover from the rain. Now that we were in the open, it really got ugly. We were about as soaked as we could be. Everything that was exposed, our shoes, socks, and hats, were wet through and through. Even with all of this going on, we were still in a good mood and having a good time.

The trail took a long turn around the airport runaway. We started to look for any hotel or hostel that might be in the area. Even though we had a reservation in Labacolla, we thought that if we saw something closer, we would jump at it. We had covered a lot of miles in very bad weather, and we wanted to get inside.

Every once and a while the rain would stop for a short time. Just when we would think we were in the clear, the bottom would drop out again. We sloshed on past the end of the airport runway into the village of San Paio. We passed a hostel that looked nice, but decided to keep going to Labacolla.

When we reached the next town, we weren't sure where we were. We stopped some young girls who were walking up the street and asked them. When they answered "Labacolla," we breathed a sigh of relief.

We followed the yellow Camino arrows for what seemed to be a long time until we saw the sign for the hostel where we had our reservation. I took a quick look at the place, and it didn't look all that great. The rain was falling so hard that we had trouble communicating. I asked Diddo if she wanted to look for a better place, and I thought that she said "yes." I started back on the trail, but she stopped me after a short distance and asked me where we were going. I was confused. I told her that I thought she said she wanted to look for a better place. She shook her head and told me that she said that the hostel looked fine and that it was listed with a three-star rating. We were yelling at each other just to hear ourselves above the rain. We both laughed at the misunderstanding and walked back to the hostel.

It turned out that the hostel was a modern place with an old wall around it. That's why it looked kind of funky to me. We went inside the walled area and up to the front door. The place looked very nice.

We were soaking wet and covered with mud, so we stopped on the front porch and started to take off our wet ponchos. The owner/manager looked out and saw us standing there. She hurried outside and pulled us into the lobby. We started to protest because we were dripping water everywhere, but she didn't want to hear any of it. She pulled our ponchos over our heads, took them into the bar, and hung them up to dry. As soon as I gave her our names, she handed us our room key and took us upstairs to our room. She told us to come back down and check in after we got dried off and rested up.

The Hostal San Paio was much nicer than we could have imagined. Warm, clean, just like heaven. The room was only 30 euros, which seemed like a great deal.

We were tired, cold, and wet to the bone. We took off our wet clothes and finally, for the first time today, started to get warm. We both took some Ibuprofen to ease our aches and pains. After a while, we got enough energy to take a shower and wash clothes. When it was my turn, I went into the bathroom and closed the door. For some reason, the door locked and I couldn't get out. I yelled to Diddo to try the door, but she couldn't open it from the outside either. We were both laughing. I was locked in the bathroom, naked, wondering what else might happen today. When we quit laughing, she slid a small screwdriver under the door, and I worked on the lock until I got it to open.

We were both starting to fade from lack of food. It was after four o'clock, so it was past the afternoon meal serving hours. We went to the restaurant to see if we could get something to eat anyway. The woman in charge told us to take a seat in the bar. After we sat down, another woman came out of the kitchen and asked us if we liked *empanadas*, to which we answered "yes." She brought us a pork *empanada*, a bottle of wine, and bottled water. The food was unbelievable, or we were very hungry. She then brought out a very large dish of seafood paella. It was so hot that it was still boiling. This all seemed like some kind of reward for staying on the Camino. This meal was so good that I can't describe it. We just sat there and ate, drank wine, and enjoyed ourselves.

This is one of our best memories of the Camino. I will never forget the hospitality, warmth, and great feeling of this place. We had come so far and been through so much. Today we had been cold, wet, tired and beat, and here, right at the end of our Camino trek, we had this great experience.

We ate until we couldn't eat any more. When we were done, we were new people. We had given up on going to the airport to check on the flights, but now that we were refreshed, we decided to head over there. The owner called a cab for us, and we took the short ride out to the airport.

During the ride, it dawned on us that we had not been in a motor vehicle of any kind for over a month. Our last ride in a car was with Jose from the Pamplona Airport to St. Jean Pied de Port. This seemed like a lifetime ago. The memories of the Camino flooded over both of us. This was an experience that we would have several times over the next few days.

When we were on the Camino, we got in the habit of getting up and going, stopping at the end of the day, taking a shower, washing clothes, eating, and sleeping. After a while, I guess we just didn't notice the miles and the days going by. Now here we were, almost at the end of the journey. This trip that we had planned and dreamed about for so long was almost at an end. We were a few short miles from Santiago, checking on flights home and riding in a car. It's hard to describe the feeling.

At the airport, we checked in at the Iberia counter. We were flying standby on Diddo's flight benefits, so it was on a space-available basis. This can get tricky, especially on international flights. The man at the counter listed us for a flight on Saturday, but our Spanish failed us when we tried to get him to check the loads. At least we were listed.

Before leaving the airport, we bought a bunch of newspapers to stuff in our boots to dry them out. When we got back to the hostel, I used the pay phone to call the Iberia 800 number. I knew that they spoke English, and I was able to check on the passenger loads. They told me that both flights, Santiago to Madrid and Madrid to Miami, were wide open on Saturday. This was good news, but you can't always rely on this information, and loads change from day to day.

We went back up to the room and cleaned everything: packs, boots, and all of our gear. Later on we went back down to the bar and just sat there and relaxed for a while before going to bed.

We had a short day ahead of us, only about six miles, with Santiago and a five-star hotel at the end. As usual, we were hoping for good weather, but at this point I think we both felt it didn't matter.

We were going to make it to Santiago!

CHAPTER 40

October 2, 2003-Thursday-Day 37
Labacolla to Santiago

6 Miles

THE big day was here, hard to believe. We were both so excited, with so many thoughts running through our heads, that we didn't sleep very well. We had such a short day ahead of us that the lack of sleep was not a big problem.

We had the alarm set for 7:00, but we were both wide-awake by 5:00. We enjoyed our stay here so much that we agreed that if we didn't like the hotel in Santiago, we would come back here. We took our time getting ready and didn't get on the trail until 8:15 a.m. Of course, it was raining and cold outside, so we put on our rain gear before heading out.

As we were walking on the trail today, everything felt great. No aches or pains. I consciously made myself enjoy every step. The memory of the first marathon we were in seems like a blur. The first time I climbed Mt. Whitney, the same. On our second marathon, I made myself enjoy the last couple of miles. I looked at the people who turned out to cheer and clap as I approached the finish. I wanted to enjoy this in the same way. Diddo was thinking the same thing. We were both quiet, lost in our own thoughts.

There was a long uphill out of Labacolla to Monte Gozo, "The Mountain of Joy." I don't think we even felt the uphill climb. There were no other pilgrims on the trail-I don't know why, maybe because of the rain. It was really coming down, and it was very cold.

From the top of Monte Gozo, we got our first real view of Santiago. The trail started downhill for a short distance to the massive *albergue* complex at Monte Gozo. We walked through the complex, which was very impressive. It has room for hundreds of pilgrims. We didn't stop. I think that we both wanted to get to the end of the trail.

We headed downhill and crossed over a freeway. There was a lot of morning traffic. I saw a sign that read "Santiago." I stopped and took a photo.

We walked a few blocks farther before it really hit us. We both stopped in our tracks and looked at each other. We were in Santiago! We had made it!

We were standing on a busy street corner in the morning rush hour and the pouring rain, hugging each other and crying. I remember seeing one of the Camino tour buses going by. Several of the occupants were looking out at us. They were smiling, waving, and pointing us out to others on the bus. The whole experience was very moving.

We started walking again, following the yellow arrows that had been our guide for the last five hundred miles. It was very cold and raining hard. The Camino never lets you take a break!

We entered the old town area, then reached the cathedral. Diddo started to cry. I just did not expect this to be such an emotional experience. Every step seemed to bring on some new feeling.

The hotel was about ten minutes away, so we decided to go to the Pilgrim's Office and get our credentials stamped and pick up our official Compostela. We found the office upstairs in a building next to the cathedral. We had to wait for a short time, still dripping with water, before we were called into the examining office. This is where they examine your credentials, confirm the information, then issue the Compostela.

The clerk gave us forms to fill out. We were so cold that we couldn't make our hands work to write the information. I had to keep blowing hot breath into my hands, and it seemed to take forever to complete the form. Diddo had the same problem. Everything checked out, so the clerk issued us our Compostela with our names written in Latin. I don't think we had worked so hard for anything in our lives.

In the outer office, before we went back outside into the rain, we tried to figure out how we were going to protect the Compostelas. After all we had been through, we didn't want them to get soaking wet. We found some papers to wrap up the documents.

We put our packs and rain gear on and headed outside. For some reason, neither one of us wanted to go into the cathedral and attend the Pilgrim's Mass. I don't know why. Maybe too much for one day. I think that we were both still in a daze. The last couple of days seemed surreal. After so long on the trail, I think that my mind just couldn't catch up to where we were.

Out on the plaza, the tourist business was going full blast. Lots of tour buses along with people milling around looking at the sights. Several people stopped us and inquired if we needed a room.

We got directions to the hotel and headed that way. It was about a ten-minute walk from the Cathedral Plaza. We found the hotel and got checked in. It was very luxurious, 125 euros a night. The clerks seemed a little stuffy, but, of course we looked like something the cat dragged in. Needless to say, the room was fantastic. We did our clothes washing and took long hot showers.

We went down to the restaurant, but found that they didn't start serving lunch until two o'clock. We must have looked like we were hungry because one of the desk clerks took us to a hospitality room where they had drinks and snacks for the hotel guests. We hung around there munching on bread and nuts until the dining room opened.

We had a fantastic meal: salad with roasted goat cheese, a big, thick, rare filet mignon smothered with grilled onions, and mashed potatoes. For dessert, apple lasagna. The meal cost 72 euros, including a bottle of wine and bottled water.

We stopped at the desk and made a reservation for the following night. We decided not to go back out today. We went to our room and started the process of cleaning our gear, packing, and getting ready for the trip home.

We called everyone at home and gave them the good news. We relaxed in a way that we had not been able to for a long time. It kept hitting us that we didn't have to do anything to get ready for the next day.

Tomorrow is a tourist day in Santiago. We don't have to hike anywhere! We can sleep in, and do whatever we want.

Later we went down to the hospitality room and had a snack. We had a cheese omelet with bacon, ice cream, and a couple of beers. We headed back to the room, happy, but still in a daze.

Pilgrim's monument at Monte Gozo

A welcome sight after 37 days on the Camino

First close look at the Cathedral

CAPITULUM hujus Almae Apostolicae et Metropolitanae Ecclesiae Compostellanae sigilli Altaris Beati Jacobi Apostoli custos, ut omnibus Fidelibus et Peregrinis ex toto terrarum Orbe, devotionis affectu vel voti causa, ad limina Apostoli Nostri Hispaniarum Patroni ac Tutelaris **SANCTI JACOBI** convenientibus, authenticas visitationis litteras expediat, omnibus et singulis praesentes inspecturis, notum facit: Dnam Eleonoram Clem hoc sacratissimum Templum pietatis causa devote visitasse. In quorum fidem praesentes litteras, sigillo ejusdem Sanctae Ecclesiae munitas, ei confero.

Datum Compostellae die 2 mensis Octobris anno Dni 2003

Secretarius Capitularis

Diddo's Compostela

CAPITULUM hujus Almae Apostolicae et Metropolitanae Ecclesiae Compostellanae sigilli Altaris Beati Jacobi Apostoli custos, ut omnibus Fidelibus et Peregrinis ex toto terrarum Orbe, devotionis affectu vel voti causa, ad limina Apostoli Nostri Hispaniarum Patroni ac Tutelaris **SANCTI JACOBI** convenientibus, authenticas visitationis litteras expediat, omnibus et singulis praesentes inspecturis, notum facit: *Dnum Jacobum Clem* hoc sacratissimum Templum pietatis causa devote visitasse. In quorum fidem praesentes litteras, sigillo ejusdem Sanctae Ecclesiae munitas, ei confero. Datum Compostellae die *2* mensis *Octobris* anno Dni *2003*.

Secretarius Capitularis

My Compostela

Some of the stamps in our Pilgrim's Credential

CHAPTER 41

October 3, 2003-Friday-Day 38
Santiago

AFTER walking 500 miles, we have a day of rest and relaxation. We both slept like rocks, and we didn't have to get up early. Woke up, went back to sleep. We didn't have to be on the trail today. What a great feeling. We took showers in the morning, just like at home. We had breakfast at the hotel restaurant, 24 euros for both of us.

We walked up to the Cathedral Plaza. The weather was cool and rainy. We walked around doing shopping for everyone at home. At a small coffee shop we ran into Buddy and Estelle. They arrived two days ago along with Bill. It was nice to sit with them and talk about the Camino and all of our experiences. We said goodbye and wished them well for the rest of their trip through Europe.

It was nice to just roam around the Plaza area, taking in the sights and being a tourist. Diddo wanted to return to a shop where she had seen something that she wanted to buy. I waited for her by the south door to the Cathedral. When she returned, I asked her if she wanted to go inside. The noon Pilgrim's Mass had just started. She said she would like that. Yesterday we avoided going to the service, but today it felt like the right thing to do. We went inside just as the priest was starting to say the prayer for all of the pilgrims. As we walked in, the splendor of the main chapel was overwhelming. I heard Diddo gasp, then start to cry. I got pretty choked up myself. The place was filled with pilgrims, many still carrying their backpacks. Some we knew, most we did not. We stayed for the remainder of the service and talked to a few of the folks that we knew.

One fellow, a Brazilian with dreadlocks, said hello. We had played trail tag with him for the last few days. He said to us in Spanish, referring to Diddo and me, "Together on the Camino, together for life." This really hit home. Doing this trip together, experiencing all of the things we had, made the memories so strong that it is hard to describe.

We sat down for a while and just took the place in. I was surprised by my feelings. Not being Catholics, I didn't think that this building would mean so much to us, but it did. While we were sitting there, Diddo told me to look up. I did and was surprised to see the symbol of the "All-Seeing-Eye," a pyramid topped by a single eye, painted on the top of the dome of the Cathedral.

We walked out through the eastern door. This leads to the street where pilgrims enter the Cathedral Plaza from the Camino. There were a few shops in this area, so we continued shopping. We went into one shop and purchased a CD with Galician music.

A weird thing happened here. Diddo started to go back up the street to another shop. This is where we had entered the plaza area yesterday as we took our last few steps on the Camino. We were just starting to walk in the opposite direction. I stopped in my tracks, which caused Diddo to stop also. She asked me what was wrong. I told her that I didn't want to walk back up the street, back onto the Camino, going the other way. I know how strange this sounds. It sounds strange to me now, sitting here writing this. But it was a very strong feeling at the time. Diddo either understood this or thought I just didn't want to do any more shopping or whatever, but she took my hand, and we turned around and headed back to the plaza area.

We took our time walking back to the hotel. We had a big, late lunch, then headed to the room to finish packing. This whole day had been very emotional but, at the same time, very nice. It was a good way to end the trek we started 38 days ago. The aches, pains, cold, rain, sore feet, and everything else, seemed to melt away. Only good feelings remained.

The hike was over, but the returning home part of the journey was in front of us. We were hoping for the best tomorrow. Our plan was to fly from Santiago to Madrid, then, with luck, from Madrid to Miami; and with a little more luck, from Miami to Las Vegas, where we planned to spend the night with our youngest daughter who was there on a temporary assignment. If we got as far as Miami, we could stay with my brother and sister-in-law. We were just hoping to be in the good old USA the following night.

Santiago Cathedral

Two happy pilgrims at the end of a long journey

CHAPTER 42

October 4, 2003-Saturday-Day 39
Santiago, Spain to Las Vegas, Nevada, USA

5800 Miles

UP early, neither one of us slept very much, too excited about going home. We took a taxi to the airport and arrived at 6:40 a.m. The airport was more crowded than I expected.

We got seats on the first flight from Santiago to Madrid. Good luck so far. This trip was only 50 minutes.

The Madrid airport is a large and very, very busy place. You stand in line forever at the ticket counters. There was a great deal of confusion about the type of standby tickets we had, which caused us to bounce from the Iberia counter to the American Airlines counter, then back to Iberia. Each time we had to stand in lines that took thirty minutes or more.

We were finally directed to a gate where an Iberia flight was about ready to leave for Miami. They told us, however, that the flight was completely full and that all of the other flights to the US were full for the rest of the day. We thought we would give it a try anyway. We took off to the boarding area, through an endless line at the security checkpoint. I had misunderstood the ticket agent and at first went to the wrong gate. Diddo pointed out this mistake, so we then headed to the right gate. It, of course, was the farthest gate from where we were.

We only had minutes before the plane took off, so we were running. We came to a second security checkpoint where they were checking passports and tickets. Each minute seemed like an hour. At one point, Diddo was ready to give in. She said, "We are never going to make it in time." We could see the gate way down at the other end of the terminal, and the last few persons were boarding. I egged her on saying, "We've got nothing to lose." We took off at a full run.

When we reached the gate, we were breathing hard and sweating. We handed the gate agent our non-rev standby tickets and asked him if they had any seats. He looked at the tickets and stated, "There are no seats on this flight" (our hearts sank until I heard the rest of the sentence) "with two seats together." He then handed us two boarding passes-not next to each other, but we were so happy to be on the flight that it didn't make any difference.

After we boarded, a very nice women sitting next to me swapped seats with Diddo, so we wound up with seats next to each other anyway. We both breathed a sigh of relief when the wheels came up. We were headed home!

It was a long trip. First Miami, a four-hour layover, then Las Vegas, where we had a short but nice visit with our daughter and son-in-law.

CHAPTER 43

October 5, 2003-Sunday-Day 40
Las Vegas, Nevada to San Diego, California

300 Miles

ON Sunday we tried to catch a flight home from Las Vegas. Unfortunately, all of the flights were jammed that day, so we got a one-way rental for $50.00 from National and drove the rest of the way.

We were so happy to be headed home that none of this bothered us in the least. We would just say to each other, "The Camino just won't let us go," then laugh. We reached our home at 10:00 p.m. on Sunday evening, very tired, but very happy.

CHAPTER 44

Epilogue

ONE of the most difficult parts of the Camino journey is returning home. This is not to say that the homecoming is not pleasant. We were both overjoyed to be home with family and friends and sleeping in our own bed. It was just the transition back into our complicated daily lives that took some getting used to.

On the trail, you are not always aware of the pleasures of living a very simple life. When you return home, the everyday complications and problems hit you head on. I thought of it as a decompression period. The thing that you miss is the simplicity of life on the Camino. Everything that you own and are responsible for, you are carrying on your back. Each day consists of simple but challenging tasks. Each day has simple but rewarding successes. I guess, in a way, being on the Camino is a break from the complications of modern-day life, a return to a more basic lifestyle that is enjoyable, at least for a while.

We were home for two weeks when a good part of Southern California started to burn. On Saturday, October 25, massive wildfires, fueled by years of tinder-dry, overgrown brush and driven by 60 mph Santa Ana winds, engulfed San Diego, Riverside, and Los Angeles Counties. For almost a week this unstoppable firestorm burned hundreds of thousands of acres of land and thousands of homes. In our small community of Alpine, over a hundred houses, many near our home, were burnt to the ground. We have several friends who lost their homes and everything they owned in the fire. This disaster had a profound effect on everyone. Whole families and communities were displaced.

During the fire, even though the area had been evacuated, we camped out at our house, with no power or telephones. We were back to the simple life whether we wanted it or not! During the first few days, the firestorm raged around our community with the unpredictable winds whipping the fire in one direction, then another. Driving around the area was like driving through Armageddon.

Driving down the freeway with no other cars in sight and both sides of the freeway walls of flame. Going into a fast-food restaurant and seeing everyone wearing face masks to filter out the smoke and ash. Going for days without seeing the sun because of the smoke. Ash everywhere and in everything. Dealing with the ash for months afterwards. These images of the firestorm will forever be burnt into our minds. We were among the lucky ones who did not suffer any loss.

About a week after the fire, we drove around San Diego County to look at the affected areas. Cuyamaca Rancho State Park, where we did most of our weekend hiking, was completely destroyed. It looked like an atom bomb had gone off. For as far as you could see, there was complete destruction. We drove for almost four hours and were always in the fire area. Time will heal the wounds caused by the firestorm of 2003, but, until then, we will be looking for other places to hike.

Things are starting to get back to normal. We are enjoying our retirement so far. I would have to say that our plan to use the Camino trip as a transition into retirement worked like a charm. We are planning our usual hiking trips, and if everything works out, we are hoping to return to the Camino in the spring of 2005.

If you are planning to hike the Camino de Santiago, we hope that our story has been helpful and inspired you to get going and get on the trail. It truly is a great adventure and the trip of a lifetime.

Buen Camino !

Good Reading

GUIDEBOOKS:

Pilgrim's Guide to the Camino Frances   John Brierley
This is the guidebook that we used. The information and maps were up to date,
and it is small enough to carry.

Walking the Camino de Santiago   Davies/Cole
Excellent guidebook, lots of good up-to-date information.

The Camino Frances   Confraternity of St. James
Outstanding, easy to carry guidebook, published every year, always up to date.

The Pilgrim's Road to Santiago   Millan Bravo Lozano
Great guidebook if you can find it. Too large to carry, and may be out of date.

The Way of St. James   Alison Raju
Small, easy to use guidebook.

BACKGROUND/HISTORY:

The Pilgrimage Road to Santiago   Gitlitz/Davidson

Lonely Planet Walking in Spain   Roddis/Placer/Fletcher/Noble

Pilgrim Stories Nancy   Louise Frey

CAMINO NARRATIVES:

On The Road to Santiago   Bob Tuggle

El Camino   Lee Hoinacki

Off the Road   Jack Hitt

Road of Stars to Santiago   Edward F. Stanton

Following the Milky Way   Elyn Aviva

My Father, My Daughter   Schell

Web Sites

Ourcamino   **www.ourcamino.com/**

Amerian Pilgrim on the Camino   **www.americanpilgrims.com/**

Canadian Company of Pilgrims   **www.santiago.ca/**

The Confraternity of Saint James   **www.csj.org.uk/**

Mundicamino.com   **www.mundicamino.com**

Spain Tourism   **www.spain.info/**

Santiago Today   **www.santiago-today.com/**

Notes

Printed in the United States
207621BV00002B/258/A